Praise for Ariel & Shya Kane – *Working on Yourself Doesn't Work*

"*#1 Best Book Buy. 10⁺ RATING! A 'must' for the library of every seeker of truth!" Awareness Magazine*

"#1 Best Seller categories." Am

"Don't let the tit about the futi effortlessness of valuable message the clarity and b

"I strongly recon experienced gui moment. The transformation meaningful and Paul English, Pub

"A great book re-examine my l much higher lev

"This warm, a transformation."

"This book is a with your friend

"The clarity and and their way o when leading m

people trapped by fire. I feel extremely fortunate to have met them."
Captain Mike Donlon
New York City Fire Department

"What the Kanes have to offer is so very simple and yet so very profound. In the garden of all the flowers for personal transformation, and I have sampled many, this is the Rose. With great love and respect, the Kanes offer keys to awareness like no one else I have ever met. Their work is truly remarkable."
Johnnie M. Jackson, Jr.
Vice President, General Counsel and Secretary, Olin Corporation

WORKING ON YOUR RELATIONSHIP DOESN'T WORK

A Transformational Approach to Creating
Magical Relationships

Ariel & Shya Kane

ASK Productions, Inc.
New York
www.ask-inc.com

Instantaneous Transformation is a registered trademark of Ariel & Shya Kane, Inc.
Magical Relationships is a trademark of ASK Productions, Inc.

Cover Design – Danielle Linares
Layout – Danielle Linares
Cover Photo – William B. Sayler
Kanes' Photo – William B. Sayler

Why Do I Worry About Silly, Silly Things?! by Amy Beth Gideon, © 2001
All Rights Reserved. Used by Permission.

Library of Congress Catalogue Card Number: 2003097887

Kane, Ariel.
    Working on your relationship doesn't work :
a transformational approach to creating magical
relationships / Ariel & Shya Kane.
    p. cm.
    LCCN 2003097887
    ISBN 1-888043-22-9

    1. Interpersonal relations. 2. Social interaction.
3. Interpersonal communication. 4. Conduct of life.
I. Kane, Shya. II. Title.

HM1106.K36 2004   158.2
                           QBI33-1667

Printed in the United States of America.
10 9 8 7 6 5 4 3 2 1

For information contact:
ASK Productions, Inc.
208 East 51st Street, PMB 137
New York, NY 10022-6500
            or
website address: http://www.ask-inc.com
email: kanes@ask-inc.com

THIS BOOK IS DEDICATED

TO ALL THOSE WHO HAVE THE COURAGE,

EVEN IN THE FACE OF DISAPPOINTMENT,

TO KEEP GOING FOR THEIR DREAMS.

WHEN YOU HAVE THE COURAGE
TO SEE YOURSELF HONESTLY
AND DO NOT JUDGE YOURSELF
FOR WHAT YOU SEE,
THEN YOUR LIFE WILL TRANSFORM
AND YOUR RELATIONSHIPS WILL
TRANSFORM ALONG WITH IT.

TRANSFORMATION IS LIKE
THE PHILOSOPHER'S STONE IN ALCHEMY
THAT WAS PURPORTED TO TURN
BASE METALS INTO GOLD.
TRANSFORMATION TAKES
AN ORDINARY, MUNDANE RELATIONSHIP
AND TURNS IT INTO A MAGICAL ONE.

PREFACE

AFTER BEING TOGETHER FOR MORE THAN 20 YEARS, OUR relationship still feels new, fresh and more intimate than ever. But there were times when it did not. When we first met, although there was a strong attraction, we related to each other in ways that were not conducive to creating a magical relationship. It wasn't that this was our intention; it was the only way we knew how to relate. Each of us did things that we had seen others do, relating as best we could. However, we were reluctant to look at those aspects of our communication and interactions that we considered to be negative. And if anything was amiss between us, it was surely the other's fault. Over the years we have discovered what it takes to build a healthy relationship and keep it alive, non-confrontational and fun. We've also learned how to sustain and rekindle the fires of love and passion.

In our first book, *Working on Yourself Doesn't Work, A Book About Instantaneous Transformation,*® we actually created the basis for having magical relationships. That book introduces our three Principles of Transformation. It outlines the difference between transforming your life and merely attempting to change those aspects with which you are not satisfied. In *Working on Your Relationship Doesn't Work, A Transformational Approach to Creating Magical Relationships,* we expand upon these ideas and principles as they apply to relationships. In this book you will find the secrets which we have stumbled upon, learned and discovered along the way, that have allowed us to move from being two individuals who were attracted to one another to a couple with a vital marriage.

Whether we are talking about a love relationship or the way in which you relate to friends, family and co-workers, the Principles of Transformation apply. They cross cultural and gender boundaries, building a strong foundation for real communication and genuine interactions to take place.

Working on Your Relationship Doesn't Work is presented with examples from our own personal experiences as a couple and as relationship coaches. You will also be transported into the midst of one of our evening seminars to get a first hand look at how a transformational approach can support you in having the relationship of your dreams.

In the *Creating the Foundation for Magical Relationships* chapter we discuss the phenomenon of transformation in depth so that you can begin to recognize it and support it happening in your life. We outline our unique perspective that will allow you to begin the process of having relationships be easier, more fun and yes — magical, too.

We will identify and explore the various corrosive elements that damage your ability to relate. These are the things that unknowingly sour intimacy, curdling what was once sweet and wholesome. Once you know of their existence, you can discover how to avoid these pitfalls.

We will also explain the principles that have helped us to rejuvenate our flagging spirits and repair the wear and tear of daily living. Some of these things you may do so naturally that you don't recognize them for the powerful relationship building tools that they are. And then, when you are off center and out of sorts with your partner, you may forget or not realize that you can employ these tools as the building blocks to reconstruct a happy, healthy, loving way of relating.

At the end of several chapters we have included simple exercises that will support you in immediately translating the ideas presented in *Working on Your Relationship Doesn't Work* from a concept into a practical experience.

Perhaps you are dating or are contemplating dating again. We share what that process was like for us and for the many we have helped to move past simply dreaming about finding a partner. We have worked with individuals who had given up on ever having a romantic relationship. They have now found their soul mates. When they applied the principles that we detail in the following pages, even people in their late thirties and forties who had never had a working relationship before have found love and lasting, exciting marriages. We have worked with others who had been married for more than three decades who have rekindled the flames of love, romance and passion after years of merely tolerating each other.

Whether you have a love that burns brightly or are still looking for that special someone, *Working on Your Relationship Doesn't Work* will help illuminate your path, allowing you to skirt the barriers to intimacy so you can have a relationship that far surpasses your dreams.

Enjoy the journey.

Ariel & Shya Kane

CREATING THE FOUNDATION
FOR A MAGICAL RELATIONSHIP

IT ALL STARTS WITH YOU

AS YOU START READING THIS BOOK, ASK YOURSELF WHY YOU HAVE
picked it up. Is it because you have heard good things about it?
Were you attracted to the title or cover? Perhaps you are stuck
somewhere on your own personal journey toward creating a
magical relationship. Or perhaps you are searching for tips to fix
your partner so that he or she is less irritating. Maybe, you are
simply curious. Any reason is valid. To get the most from what
Working on Your Relationship Doesn't Work has to offer, it is
important that you begin to know yourself.

2

Since you have picked up this book, chances are you are interested in having relationships that are rewarding to you and to the people with whom you relate. In the following pages, you are likely to come across things that you do and have done naturally all along that work well in your dealings with others. You will also identify things that are impediments to your ability to have a day-to-day sense of well-being. Both are important.

The ideas presented in this book are a radical departure from working on yourself or your relationship to bring about positive change. This book is about discovering a new way of seeing, a new way of looking at yourself, your life and your relationships. It will require you to learn a few very simple principles that can shift the way you relate, and the way you think about your life.

The two of us have found a far faster and more lasting approach than that of picking on oneself and one's partner and making endless lists of resolutions designed to force ourselves to behave in a more positive manner. We have discovered the possibility of transformation.

WHAT IS TRANSFORMATION?

Let's start with a brief introduction to what is meant when we use the term transformation. Transformation is a phenomenon that we will be exploring over the course of this book. This is only the initial foray into an explanation of this complex, yet simple happening.

Transformation is a shifting in the essence of something. For example, a molecule of water goes from a liquid to a solid at 32 degrees Fahrenheit. Even though its molecular structure has stayed the same, ice does not resemble water because it has transformed.

TRANSFORMATION IS SIMPLY A WORD WE USE
TO DESCRIBE WHAT HAPPENS WHEN YOU DISCOVER
HOW TO LIVE IN THE MOMENT.

It is a shifting of the way you interact with life so that mechanical, automatic, unaware behaviors cease to dominate your choices. Transformation might be equated to a proactive way of life but not in opposition to anything. Most people have determined their lives either in agreement or opposition to something they have experienced or have been exposed to. In transformation, the circumstances of your life may stay the same but the way you relate to those circumstances radically shifts. Before people's lives transform, they blame their circumstances for how they feel. However, after transformation takes place, circumstances are no longer the determining factor. It is a state where the mere seeing of a behavior pattern is enough to complete it. Transformation affects all aspects of a person's life, not merely one area. It is not produced by will or a desire to transform. It happens to a person and it happens when a person lives life directly rather than thinking about how to live life the 'right way'. Transformation is the natural outcome when you bring awareness to your life.

AWARENESS

Our definition of awareness is a non-judgmental seeing. It is an objective, non-critical seeing or witnessing of the nature or 'isness' of any particular circumstance or situation. It is an ongoing process in which you are training yourself to bring yourself back to the moment rather than complaining in your thoughts about what you perceive as wrong or about what you would prefer.

Most of us have been taught that when we become aware of something, we then have to do something to change or fix what we discover. With transformation, awareness itself is often enough to facilitate resolution without doing anything about what is seen.

You could equate it to walking through a large conference hall with the lights turned off. If there were chairs and tables strewn about and you attempted to cross the room directly, you would undoubtedly stumble or fall. However, with light, you could easily avoid all of the obstacles. Merely by illuminating what is, those pitfalls that stand in the way of having a harmonious relationship can be circumvented.

AN ANTHROPOLOGICAL APPROACH

Our approach is anthropological in nature. Rather than concerning ourselves with why people are the way they are, we are interested in seeing the mechanics and dynamics of how people function. An anthropologist suspends judgment to study cultures objectively, not as right or wrong, good or bad, or as something that needs to be fixed or changed, but simply to see their social mores, customs and standards. He or she observes how a culture operates and interacts. We invite you to investigate your way of relating through this anthropological metaphor. Be a scientist and study a culture of one — yourself.

6

In order to create a magical relationship, it is important that you learn the art of self-observation without self-reproach. Most of us do not simply observe how we function. Rather, we judge ourselves, comparing how we are to how we think we ought to be based on cultural standards (or the resistance to those standards). We are addicted to fixing what we perceive as our weaknesses and faults rather than observing ourselves neutrally. Transformation is not about fixing yourself to be a better you or fixing your partner to be a new improved version of himself or herself. It is about being the way you are. If you simply see how you are without judging, manipulating or trying to fix what is seen, this will facilitate the completion of unwanted behaviors.

How? Well, neutrally observing something doesn't add energy to it — for or against — and everything in this universe needs energy to survive. If you don't energize your habits, they will naturally dwindle and die away all on their own.

It took the two of us many years to discover how to relate in a way that allowed our relationship to flower and grow, be nurturing and deepen. We stumbled upon the answer one day while walking up a hill from a beach in San Francisco. It was in that moment that Shya realized he was done working on himself. Shortly thereafter he stopped picking on Ariel as well.

IF YOU WANT TO HAVE A SOUL MATE
AND NOT AN OPPONENT IN A NEVER-ENDING FIGHT,
THE PLACE TO BEGIN IS WITH YOURSELF.
IF YOU ARE PICKING ON YOURSELF,
YOU WILL PICK ON YOUR PARTNER.
THE TWO OF US HAVE TRULY DISCOVERED
THAT WORKING ON YOURSELF
(AND YOUR RELATIONSHIP) DOESN'T WORK.

AGREEING AND DISAGREEING

Please hold in abeyance the tendency to agree or disagree with the ideas being presented because if you pick them apart you will never get the essence of what is being said. This is because if you are agreeing or disagreeing, you are comparing what is being said to what you already know rather than really listening. Part of the technology of transformation is to train yourself to listen to the point of view of the speaker rather than think about whether or not you agree or disagree with what is being said. In this case, the written word is the speaker.

To discover something new, you must give up the idea that you already know what is being said. You also have to move past the fear of looking stupid, either to yourself or to others, for not already knowing what you discover. Our request is that you give it a chance. What we are talking about works. It has been proven in the lives of those people who have mastered the principles in this book. Please know that we appreciate the courage it takes, and we know the discomfort that one goes through, in learning any new skill-set and learning the skill-set of awareness is no exception.

AGENDAS

Many people will be reading this book with an agenda to fix something that is wrong with their partner. When this is the case, they will focus in on the sections that they feel address their partner's 'problems' and will disregard anything that does not support what they are proving to be true. People gather evidence to support their points of view and disregard anything that does not support them. Take for instance the woman who has the idea that men are crude, rude and insensitive oafs. Any time a man is kind, gentle or nice to her, these behaviors are disregarded. It is not that she thinks to dismiss them; it is as though there is a filter that sifts out anything that does not support her point of view. As you read on, we will explore the subject of agendas in more depth. This will support you in becoming aware of your own personal filters, which were created by a less expanded, younger version of yourself. Your agendas limit what is possible for you.

CONFUSION AND PARADOX

There are two factors in a transformational approach that need to be talked about. The first is confusion. Since this approach is so outside the commonly held reality regarding relationships, confusion will be a common response. This is not a problem. It is part of the process when the mind grapples with new ideas.

The second factor is paradox, which happens when there are two seemingly conflicting or contradictory ideas, which both actually true. A classic example of paradox would be the statement: "Water, water everywhere and not a drop to drink." These are two seemingly contradictory statements but if you have ever seen a river after it has overflowed its bank in a flood, then you know that these two statements are both possible at the same time. In a flood situation there is water everywhere but you certainly wouldn't want to drink it.

Here is a story that illustrates paradox:

Once a master and his servant were crossing a desert. They came to an oasis and decided to spend the night. In the morning they awoke to discover that their camels were gone. The master said to his servant "Where are the camels?"

To which the servant replied, "Well, I just did what you always tell me to do."

"What is that?" asked the master.

"You always tell me to trust in Allah, so that is what I did. I trusted Allah would take care of the camels."

"Ahh," the master replied. "This is true. Of course, you must trust in Allah but you also must tether the camels."

The paradox in a transformational approach to creating a magical relationship is that there is nothing to do with what you discover and sometimes there are things that need to be done.

LEARNING SOMETHING NEW

What needs to be addressed next is how the mind works. It operates much like a computer, sorting information by similarities or differences to what it already knows. This is a very useful function, however, it can also work as an impediment to discovering anything that exists outside the known.

Our minds function by extrapolating from our past. They can only suggest possible futures based on what is already known. So, if you have never had a good relationship, to conceive of a great one is impossible. It is much more difficult to see what you don't already know because the mind is likely to fill in with past information and knowledge that colors the moment. Take, for example, the following expression:

PARIS IN THE
THE SPRING

'Paris in the spring' is an old saying that you may have heard many times. But, when you read the statement above, did you notice anything out of the ordinary? Did you see that in fact this quote had an error? It actually reads Paris in <u>the the</u> Spring. The mind sees what it is expecting to see and often overlooks what is really there. It will rearrange what is actually being said to fit its logic system.

If you read this book to see if you agree or disagree with what is being said, you will miss what is new because you can only agree or disagree from comparing what is said to what you already know. You will be inadvertently reinforcing all the ways you currently relate, including those aspects of your relationships that you find distressing.

THE PRINCIPLES OF TRANSFORMATION

There is a possibility of having truly magical relationships in all aspects of your life, whether it is a romantic relationship, one with family or friends or simply your relationship to yourself.

It is our hypothesis that if the Principles of Transformation are applied to relationship, the result will be partnership, self-expression and self-fulfillment. Again, we suggest that you hold in abeyance the tendency to agree or disagree with these principles and merely hold them as a possibility through which one can examine the complexities of relationship.

There are three Principles of Transformation.

THE FIRST PRINCIPLE IS: ANYTHING YOU RESIST PERSISTS AND GROWS STRONGER.

Have you noticed that if there is something about your partner you don't like or have tried to change, the more you have worked to fix or change him or her, the more he or she has persisted in staying the same? Those things that you disagree with about your partner dominate your life and your relationship. Eventually, those are the only things you focus on. You no longer see the good points, those things that attracted you to him or her in the first place. You only see faults or what you consider to be his or her faults. So again, the first principle is anything you resist will persist, will continue and will in fact dominate your relationship.

THE SECOND PRINCIPLE IS:
NO TWO THINGS CAN OCCUPY
THE SAME SPACE AT THE SAME TIME.

Another way of looking at this might be that in any given instant, you can only be the way you are. Most people have the idea that they could be different than they are or that their lives could have been different than they were. But if you look and tell the truth about what you see, you will discover that in any given moment you can only be exactly the way you are.

Here is an example:
If we were to take a camera and photograph you, when the camera's shutter opens, you are captured exactly as you are in that instant of time and in that moment, you could not be any different than you were when the film captured your image. You may think that you could have been different, but in reality, that moment has already gone by and nothing can be done to change it. Therefore, it could only have happened the way it did and you could only have been the way you were. In your fantasies you can construct lots of alternative possibilities to how you were when the camera's shutter opened and closed but in reality, you could have only been the way you were. Most of us do not

realize that our lives are made up of a series of moments that could not have been different than they were.

What we are suggesting is that you cannot be different than you are in any given moment and everything that has ever happened in your life could only have happened that way because it did. This principle, if truly seen, will release you from a lifetime of regret and guilt.

THE THIRD PRINCIPLE OF TRANSFORMATION IS: ANYTHING YOU ALLOW TO BE EXACTLY AS IT IS, WITHOUT TRYING TO CHANGE OR FIX IT, WILL COMPLETE ITSELF.

This means that the mere seeing of an unwanted behavior is enough to facilitate resolution. This principle may be a little more difficult to grasp than the other two. The idea of merely seeing something, rather than doing something about what you see, seems wrong or incomplete or as if it won't accomplish anything. But, let's go back to the conference hall analogy for a moment. Again, let's suppose you want to cross a room filled with tables and chairs. If it is dark, you will surely bump into the obstacles. With light you can cross the room in a natural manner.

As you walk through the living room of your home each day, you don't have to remind yourself not to stumble over the couch. It is something that is included in your awareness and your actions take into account that this piece of furniture occupies space. You don't work on effectively crossing the room to avoid collision with the furniture. It is naturally, immediately integrated into your way of being. The chairs or couch become the background rather than the focus of your attention. So it is with your mechanical behaviors. If you notice you have them without resisting what you see, they lose their power over your life.

Here is another practical example that demonstrates all three principles:

Once the two of us went to a Mexican restaurant in New York's Greenwich Village. The restaurant was an intimate little place near a local hospital. After the waitress seated us and we ordered, we noticed that two tables over a group of young doctors were having a meal. From the gist of their conversation, we discovered that they were all fairly new residents. One fellow was particularly loud. He talked about where he went to school, about the senior resident, Dr. Cho, and as he went along, he carried on an increasingly animated conversation about the woman with ulcers and the man with kidney stones whom he had seen on that morning's rotation. The more the two of us tried to distance ourselves from his annoying monologue, the louder and more intrusive it became. Soon our worldview shrank to being dominated by our resistance to the conversation at this nearby table. Eventually, our orders came and we began to eat and chat about our plans for the day. Just when we were finishing the last of our meal, we realized that not only had the fellow stopped talking but, unbeknownst to us, he and his colleagues had paid their check and left the restaurant.

Let's look at the anecdote through the Principles of Transformation: When we first got to the restaurant, expecting to have a quiet lunch, we definitely resisted the fellow who was not only talking to the other doctors at his table but also loud enough to be disturbing to other patrons. We resisted not only the volume but also the content of what he had to say. By disagreeing with the fact that he was a part of our lunch, behaving as he was, his presence dominated our experience of the moment. This was the first principle: What you resist persists and grows stronger — or in this case talks louder. It also involved the second principle: No two things can occupy the same space at the same time. When we had our attention fixed on him, he consumed our thoughts.

At some point during our meal, the third principle came into play. We didn't decide to ignore the loud fellow and concentrate on topics of our choosing. We weren't trying to avoid thoughts of ulcers and kidney stones. This would have been a form of resisting the moment that would have had us back where we started. We just put our attention on each other and our meal. In other words, we didn't try to change or fix the situation or our irritation. We allowed the situation and our response to be exactly the way it was without judging him or ourselves. We also didn't act out or express our irritation. And the situation resolved itself. When we took our attention away from our complaints, the doctors had paid their bill and left the restaurant, unnoticed. When you allow something to be exactly the way it is, it allows you to be.

IF YOU WANT A MAGICAL RELATIONSHIP, START WITH YOURSELF

Most people focus on their partner as the source of their dissatisfaction and disharmony. In a transformational approach it is always your responsibility for how your relationship is going. Our way of looking at it is to bring awareness to yourself and what you are doing or not doing that is straining or stressing the relationship. Please note that responsibility is not the same as saying problems are your 'fault'. Responsibility is being willing to acknowledge that what happens in your relationship happens around you and that there is a way you are being or operating that is producing what you say you don't like.

When we work with couples, we treat their relationship as though it is not a 50/50 deal. When we're speaking to one partner, we speak to that person as if the dynamic is 100% his or her responsibility. When we switch focus to the second person, we speak to that partner as if the responsibility for the dynamic is 100% his or hers. We have found this an empowering way to look at how people relate because even if you were to have a different partner, your mechanical way of relating would very likely trigger the same type of scenario and 'problems' that you have created in your current or past relationships.

In your relationship there is not the 'good' person and the 'bad' person. The dynamics are generated between both of you. We often think of it like Velcro. Velcro is made of two sides, hooks and fluff. You need both in order to have something join. If you don't have fluff, then the hooks won't stick. And if you don't have hooks then the fluff has nothing to snag.

YOUR RELATIONSHIP WITH YOURSELF
DETERMINES YOUR RELATIONSHIP
WITH YOUR PARTNER

If you want to have your relationship grow and be nurturing after love's first blush, it is important to first take a look at your relationship to yourself. In our most private thoughts the majority of us are very hard on ourselves. We are our own most critical critics, finding fault with ourselves and thinking we should do our lives differently or better. There is an old Groucho Marx line that says, "I wouldn't belong to any club that would have me as a member." This saying is humorous mainly because it is so honest and reflective of the truth for so many.

Here is how thinking negatively about yourself directly impacts your relationship:

Let's say when you are being self-critical and judgmental you think of yourself as: less, wrong, stupid, inept, unsophisticated, fat, too old or unattractive, etc. Then, if someone finds you attractive, this person has a major strike against him or her simply by the act of being attracted to you with all of your 'faults'. It stands to reason that if you don't like yourself, then from this same logic system, the person who finds you attractive must be deficient somehow or at the very least has bad taste and judgment. When you are hard on yourself, you are hard on any person related to you. If you demean yourself in your thoughts, you will by association transfer that way of relating to your partner and relationship. If you are out to fix your shortcomings, that new person in your life is destined to sooner or later become your next fixer-upper project. You will begin to try and change and fix them to get them to behave the right way, molding them to your ideal person much the same way you try to mold yourself.

IF YOU WANT TO BUILD
A RESPECTFUL, KIND AND LOVING RELATIONSHIP,
YOU MUST BEGIN WITH BEING
RESPECTFUL, KIND AND LOVING TO YOURSELF.

E X E R C I S E S

CREATING THE FOUNDATION
FOR A MAGICAL RELATIONSHIP

The following exercises are the opportunity to begin investigating your life through an anthropological/transformational framework. If you feel to do them, see if you can do so without judging yourself for what you discover. If you simply see how you are without judging, manipulating or trying to fix what is seen, this will facilitate the completion of unwanted behaviors and conditions.

1.   Find examples in your own life to illustrate the three Principles of Transformation.

2.   Notice how you talk about yourself in the privacy of your own thoughts.

3.   Notice how often you agree and disagree while listening to another person.

HOW YOU DO ANYTHING IS HOW YOU DO EVERYTHING

DISCOVERING YOUR RELATIONSHIP DNA

START WITH THE IDEA THAT HOW YOU DO ANYTHING IS HOW YOU do everything and it will empower you to investigate how you relate, not just in a love relationship, but also with yourself and all others. This defuses the mindset of looking to fix what is 'broken' and sets you on the path to having magical relationships in all areas of your life.

Your DNA is unique and in every cell of your body. The way you relate to life and to others is also unique to you. The way you operate is predictable so it will repeat itself over and over again. Of course, there will be instances when you do not react as you usually do, but if you look at the overall pattern of your behavior, you will start to identify these predictable, recurring ways of relating. In other words, in certain situations with certain types of people, you usually respond the same way.

Using our anthropological/transformational approach, if you become aware of the way you function, behaviors that have heretofore interfered with or destroyed relationships can be identified. Then the Principles of Transformation again come into play. If you realize that you can only have related the way you did until you became aware of your behaviors (Second principle) and if you do not judge what you see, these mechanical behaviors will complete themselves (Third principle), creating the possibility for magical relationships. Of course, if you resist what you discover, this will reinforce your automatic, reflexive behaviors and keep them around (First principle).

NO MATTER WHERE YOU GO, THERE YOU ARE

People have the idea that if they change their location, it will change their lives, but this is not the case.

Here is an example:

Jack[1] moved from Colorado to New York to get away from a dead-end job, difficulties with his associates and a relationship that was going nowhere. Within 5 months, he had alienated most of the people who had befriended him upon his arrival and had subsequently quit his new place of employment. Jack thought the dating scene in New York was brutal; everyone was totally unfair and he needed a change. He picked up and moved to Texas. In this new location things turned from bad to worse. He started a new business and quickly got into legal troubles. After a long and costly series of dealings with the law, he promised to change his ways and the authorities let him go with a mere 'slap on the wrist'. So on Jack went to California where he started the same type of business with another dubious partner and he immediately got into similar troubles with business associates as well as with the California State and Federal authorities.

Even though he changed his location, Jack kept creating basically the same circumstances. The same scenario kept recurring wherever he went. People initially liked him, went out of their way to support him and were always disappointed when his true

---

1 The names in the anecdotes and examples used throughout *Working on Your Relationship Doesn't Work* have been changed to preserve privacy and anonymity.

colors became apparent. Even though he met new people in these different places, somehow he managed to create the same outcome, over and over.

Of course, Jack's story is an extreme example. But, it typifies how personal patterns follow people wherever they go. Have you ever noticed that similar interpersonal dynamics between you and others develop over and over? This is not to suggest that you shouldn't move or find a new boyfriend or girlfriend. What we are suggesting is that the most exciting journey is the one of self-discovery. When you know yourself and are able to dissolve the mechanical responses to your life, then the primary person you are relating to, you, will be an excellent companion.

TRANSFORMATION DISSOLVES
THE REPETITIVE NATURE OF LIFE

We had a participant come to one of our winter retreats who was a victim of spousal abuse, having been hit, bitten and beaten. Even the family pet had been threatened with bodily harm. Jim had a wife, Rita, who was abusive. She would regularly fly into a rage and had once even physically attacked a motorist whom she found offensive.

Jim finally found the courage to dissolve this marriage. Rita wasn't going to change. She was unwilling to be responsible for her anger and how she expressed it.

So Jim found a new relationship. It started well but shortly, he discovered that he wasn't any happier. His new partner was not physically abusive but communications between them broke down and physical intimacy was rare. Soon Jim discovered that his partner was having affairs.

Life moved on and eventually Jim met and fell in love with the woman who is now his wife. Although Jim and his wife, Dahlia, are happily married and have been for years, at first, the seeds for disharmony were there.

In the early stages of all three relationships Jim was excited, attentive and loving. As the weeks and months progressed, his habitual way of relating emerged and he became frantic at work, stressed, less communicative and his partners each felt neglected. Resentments grew, intimacy ended and Jim and his mate would fight.

Because we were a part of Jim's life during all three relationships, we were able to see that he related in a similar manner with all three partners. However, each of these three people dealt with the stresses of his mechanical way of relating with mechanical, reactive behaviors of their own.

His first wife had a violent predisposition and his way of being evoked her rage. His second partner was more quietly aggressive and the way they related resulted in promiscuous behavior. Dahlia has a different predisposition. When upset, she traditionally becomes quiet, clingy, insecure and depressed. She would want to stay home every night and resented the time that Jim gave to anyone, even his clients.

Here is how Jim and Dahlia went from having a normal, quietly unhappy relationship to creating a great one:

First, each of them realized that when upset, they had ways of relating that were not conducive to creating a magical relationship. With our coaching, Dahlia spoke up about what was bothering her and Jim actually listened without defending himself. He didn't judge himself for how he was being and interestingly enough, Dahlia didn't judge him either. She just wanted him to hear her, to know how she felt. She wanted *him,* the man she fell in love with, not the frenzied fellow he had become.

Actually, all three of Jim's partners wanted his attention and they all had different ways of expressing their displeasure. We are not saying that Jim *caused* the violence, the affairs or the depression of his partners. What we are saying is that your unexamined behavior patterns will link up with your partner's mechanics and produce mischief.

Should you stay in a relationship that is violent, for instance, because you have evoked unfinished business in your partner? Of course not. Our point is that your partner is not behaving badly in a vacuum. As we said before, there is no good one and no bad one in a relationship. As Jim became aware of the mechanical ways in which he distanced himself from his partners both emotionally and physically, then he and Dahlia were able to finally express and live from the passion they had for one another and their passion for life.

NOW THAT YOU HAVE A BASIC INTRODUCTION TO transformation, awareness and our anthropological approach to relationship, we will transport you to one of our New York City Monday evenings as written from Ariel's point of view. Come ride along and immerse yourself in transformation and relationship from our perspective. In the light and easy format of our seminars, people have discovered personal well-being and have transformed their ability to relate. Join us as we meet some amazing people and see the natural unfolding that is a hallmark of true transformation.

The Monday evening meeting was really beginning to cook. As I looked around to scan the faces and survey what was happening, I smiled to myself. It was hard to believe that only one hour ago, Shya and I had been standing outside enjoying the balmy air of an Indian Summer evening. On the horizon, the sky had been fading to that really dark indigo blue which I have loved ever since I was a child. Sometimes it still surprises me that even between Manhattan's tall buildings, the beauty of a night sky can grab my heart and give it a gentle tug.

Soon after admiring the sky, Shya and I had walked into the building and went into the auditorium we had been renting for these weekly seminars. As the room began to fill with participants, I felt a light breath on the left side of my neck and my body responded with goose bumps rippling down my left side. Smiling, I turned to give Shya a squeeze and appreciated his new haircut.

We had gone to our friend and master hair cutter, Michael, that day because it was time to get a trim. As Shya sat in the chair, covered with a big plastic apron to catch the shorn hair, Michael had been grappling with what exactly it is that we do in our workshops.

"Is it like The est Training or like The Landmark Forum?" Michael asked while performing a particularly neat feathering cut on the top shock of hair on Shya's head.

"No, it is not like est or Landmark at all. I guess you could see some similarities if you looked through a system that was based in est but then again, if you looked through a system that was based in psychotherapy, it would look like psychotherapy, or if your background was based in Zen it would look like Zen."

"We even had someone compare us once to Amway," I added with a grin.

Michael looked at me incredulously, "But Amway is a company that sells household products. How can anyone even think to compare what you do to that?" he asked rather indignantly in his rich French accent.

"Well actually, Michael, it isn't so strange a comparison," Shya continued flashing a grin back in my direction, *Ariel, you're really mischievous today. You got him going.* "See, people can only draw upon what they know. Let's look at it this way. You know everything that you know, right?"

"Yes." Michael resumed feathering.

"But, you also don't know everything that you don't know. So when I tell you about our transformational seminars, the natural process for your mind is to understand. Your mind will fit what I say into a framework it already knows and is comfortable with. It just simply deletes the nuances of what it doesn't know and puts in what it assumes is the reasonable facsimile."

Shya looked thoughtful for a moment before continuing. "My father used to like to sing nursery rhymes to me. I grew up by the ocean in Far Rockaway, NY and I loved it when he would take me by the hand down to the seaside. By the time I was five or so, I used to like to watch the people in the ocean on hot summer days and my dad would sing 'My body lies over the ocean. My body lies over the sea. My body lies over the ocean. Oh, bring back my body to me.' It was one of my favorite songs."

Michael began chuckling as he reached for his electric razor to clean up some of the fine hairs on the back of Shya's neck.

"Several years later I discovered that the true lyrics were, 'my bonnie lies over the ocean', but as a youngster, a 'bonnie' wasn't in my vocabulary yet. What Ariel and I do has a flavor that is uniquely our own. If our work were based in anything, it would be based in not punishing yourself for being yourself and not having to change or fix yourself to try to fit some kind of ideal you've been taught as to how you are supposed to be. We have discovered that, when a person gets into the moment, his or her life transforms – instantaneously."

"Do you prepare for your groups?"

"There are certain workshops, such as our business courses, which we outline but even so, we leave room to be inspired by the participants themselves. If we didn't take into consideration who was coming, it would be like planning on baking a cake without knowing what ingredients were being delivered to the kitchen."

Later that Monday night, when Shya murmured in my ear "Looks like our cake is arriving Ariel," I had fun looking at the 'ingredients' who were showing up.

As I saw friends, acquaintances and new faces round the corner and enter the lobby, I chuckled to myself as I imagined all of us entering the room for the evening as if it were the oven and we would all be baked when we emerged and yet none of us knew what was on the menu.

7:30 rolled around and it was time to begin. Shya and I took our places in the tall director's chairs that made it easier to see and be seen by all. An expectant hush fell over the room.

"Good Evening. I'm Ariel for those of you we haven't met,"

"And I am Shya. Welcome to our Instantaneous Transformation evening. Tonight, it is possible to open the door to living in the moment and discover how to have a truly satisfying life. Tonight is designed to allow you to discover and dissolve those mechanical behaviors that rob you of spontaneity, joy, creativity and relationship. The theme tonight is Instantaneous Transformation. Ariel and I have discovered that when you get into the moment, your life transforms. And by transformation we mean a quantum shift in all aspects of your life, a shift where you are returned to a sense of well-being and you are able to respond effectively and appropriately to your environment. By the simple act of awareness, which is an observing without judging what you see about yourself or others, it is possible to melt the barriers to happiness, fulfillment and satisfaction."

Many folks began to nod their heads in agreement with Shya's words. His description was consistent with their experience of transformation. I also noticed a number of new folks who were beginning to acquire that intense look that seems to come along when the mind is sorting out a particularly difficult problem. I could relate to the disorientation I read on many of the faces. I imagine I looked similarly when I first learned to use a personal computer.

As I had sat in front of the Macintosh screen that blustery November morning, I felt so inept. There were words that I thought I knew. They were supposedly in the English language, but even so they made only limited sense. I found the manual, with its new application of old familiar words, daunting. "Take the mouse and drag it across the mouse pad to move the cursor on your screen," it had read. The only mouse I had been familiar with had been the little gray and white kind with the quivery whiskers of my childhood and surely anything that cursed on a screen should be censored. And even when I did understand the concepts and the new usage for these words, my mouse clicking skills left a lot to be desired at first. Now, it is hard to remember what it is like not to use a computer but at first, I had to embrace learning something new.

So as I looked at the faces of those in front of us, I had compassion for the process of rediscovering familiar words used in a new context.

"There are actually things that you can do that will keep you from being in the moment," Shya continued.

"And we are going to tell you what they are so that you can do them if you wish to avoid the phenomenon of Instantaneous Transformation," I finished and smiled. Folks shifted in their chairs laughing appreciatively.

In the front row, Shya saw an earnest face looking back at him. An attractive African-American woman in her mid thirties sat with pen poised, ready to record the main points.

"Hi, what's your name?"

The woman checked behind herself to make sure he had been addressing her. "Vanessa."

"Hi, Vanessa. It's nice to see that you are here obviously looking to get the most from the evening."

Vanessa's shoulders gave a hint of relaxing.

"May I make a suggestion?"

She nodded. "We recommend that you don't take notes."

Vanessa smiled a brilliant smile and lowered her pen.

"See, taking notes will take you away from here. You will be collecting data or information to apply to your life later to fix what you think has been wrong with it in the past. You can't work on yourself to have your life transform. Remember, we said that just getting into this moment is enough. In order to take notes, you have to abridge, translate and write down what is said to an understandable format for later. But, what is of use here tonight is not easily understood."

"For instance, you can understand what makes a sunset become a brilliant red, but understanding is not the same as the intensity of the experience. Perhaps you can just 'hang out', relax and see what happens. If you get present, you won't need any written pointers or guidelines or tips to take away from tonight."

"See, Vanessa, this brings us to the second thing that will keep people from being in the moment, their agendas. An individual's ideas and goals of what they want severely limits the infinite possibilities that life has to offer because they will scan for what they think is needed in order to be happy and filter out so many other rich and varied things. When a person is striving for something, it is usually based on the idea that what they have now is insufficient or what they did in the past is wrong. It's funny, we've seen people come to our groups hungry for a job or to get a relationship or to have more fun in their lives, to name but a few agendas, and they are so serious about these goals, that they miss this moment. And in this moment, an available attractive person may be sitting nearby but will be overlooked in the act of seeking. Others have literally talked the potential employer sitting next to them out of offering them a job because the out-of-work individual was so busy trying to get ahead that they disregarded the person who had jobs to offer. You would be amazed at the number of people who are actually being serious about their search for fun. See if you can be here tonight and let go of trying to get ahead."

Vanessa nodded thoughtfully. I could tell she was a little reluctant but she was game to give it a go. Bending down she placed her pen and pad under her chair so she wouldn't be tempted and would be free to be there. As she sat up, Vanessa graced us with another brilliant and infectious smile. I appreciated that smile and also the fact that she had let that pad, her pen and the idea to take notes really go. She took our suggestion and made it her own. Transformation was already happening here. Vanessa may have been reluctant at first but by the time she sat back up, she was truly there.

I shifted my focus to include the entire room. "We suggest you listen. And by that we mean *really* listen – not only to us but also to whatever anyone has to say. Get interested. Invest yourself in being here with totality. Watch where your mind wants to wander off, as if what is happening in your life in this moment, is not important. Notice if you take exception to a word in order to miss the essence of what is being said."

"Most people think that they are listening when what they are really doing is completely different. Frequently people are actually agreeing or disagreeing. When you agree or disagree, you take what is being said and compare it to what you know, to the knowledge you have gathered from the past. Depending on what is in your knowledge bank, you will say to yourself, *Yes, that is true,* or *No, I don't agree with that.* But this takes you out of the moment. You will naturally agree and disagree with things as the evening progresses. It's a normal, automatic function of our minds. So don't make yourself wrong or chastise yourself when you see it happening. Just bring your attention, your awareness back to what is being said and that is all you need to do."

"Speaking of comparison," I segued, "comparison is another function that will take you out of here. How many of you have ever read self-help books, articles, meditated, taken a personal growth class or gone to therapy?" Almost everyone raised his or her hand and as I looked around, I noticed a man in the front who was slumped down looking as if he were there under duress. This was just another weird evening that his girlfriend, who was sitting on his left, had dragged him to. She was nudging him to get him to raise his hand because she had taken him with her to many different events but there was no budging.

"Your mind compares. We will say things tonight that may sound similar to things you have heard before because you all have a handicap. You are smart. And smart people, people who have worked on themselves, have the hardest time hearing things newly. In Zen they have a saying called the beginner's mind. See if you can be willing tonight to let go of what you know and be here as if for the first time."

"Let's see, what else will take you out of the moment," I said, looking at Shya and then looking out to those assembled there because for now, I had run out of steam. There was a pause as we all contemplated the question.

"Proving and defending," a familiar voice from the right side prompted. Shya and I smiled in unison at Roger. His comment had come from a rich background with us and he was willing to share with others his expertise, even at the risk of looking foolish. Roger has bright red hair, freckles, a dimple in his chin and is one of our dearest friends as well as our C.P.A. and money manager.

"Go ahead and explain what you mean by proving and defending," Shya said, giving him the challenge because he knew the story that Roger was about to relate. Immediately we were touched because our friend was about to reveal the foibles of his youth, the much lesser version of himself from more than 15 years earlier when his business was young.

"Well," Roger began with a good natured grin, "if you are here to prove anything, such as how smart you are, how you know better than Ariel and Shya do, then you will miss being here this evening. Actually, I am very familiar with defending or protecting a point of view. See, I am Ariel and Shya's accountant..."

As Roger began to unashamedly tell his story, the morning he was referring to came into focus in my mind's eye. We met with Roger that day because Shya and I had decided that from now on, when possible, we would not spend money before we actually earned it. People often paid their tuition for our groups in advance and we had gotten into the habit of spending the money as it came in. Our concern was that if for some reason people's plans changed or we had to cancel an event for some unforeseen reason, we would not have the money to give back. We did not want to have to manipulate people to be in our groups because we had already spent their money. Shya and I had the idea to put payments for groups into an escrow account and only release the funds to ourselves once we had actually earned them.

Enthusiastically we told Roger of the plan. He didn't understand it. We explained it again. Still he looked dumbly at us. I tried to explain the concept again in very plain terms, kind of like those story problems I had hated in math class as a child. I knew that this explanation would work. I was excited.

"Hang on Shya, let me give him a great example," I said, confident that this would do the trick. "Ready?" Roger nodded. "Joe pays us for a workshop which he totally plans to attend. We spend the money. Two days later, Joe's mother unexpectedly falls ill and he has to fly out to California to be with her. He misses the course. We want to refund his tuition, but we have already spent the money. Had we known better, we would have held his money aside, in case there was an emergency, so that we could give him a refund. Only after Joe actually completed a course with us, would the money he had paid be ours because, by then, we would have earned it." I sat back rather proud of myself. The morning sun reflected off the glass-topped table. I waited for Roger's face to clear but he still stared at me as if I were speaking a foreign language.

I couldn't believe my eyes. Was this the brilliant man we knew and loved? Was this the fellow who had majored in accounting, had worked for a big accounting firm and finally had become a Certified Public Accountant after passing the rigorous C.P.A. exam?

All of a sudden, Shya started laughing and his laughter deepened into a belly laugh. "I get it. I get it. I finally figured it out," he said. Roger looked a little nervous that he may find out something that would make him feel even more inept, but at the same time he looked relieved because by now we had been trying to explain this concept for over an hour. "Roger, tell me, how do we pay you?"

"Uhh, by check," he replied, mystified.

"But, do we pay you an hourly rate, by the day, what?"

"Oh, that's simple to answer. I get 6% of Ariel's and your gross income in exchange for doing your bookkeeping, taxes, paying the bills, keeping your workshop records and making deposits, etc."

Although Roger had answered Shya's question, it didn't give him any relief. He still remained in a stupor, but I was beginning to see the joke.

"And tell me Roger," Shya continued, "When do you pay yourself your 6%?"

"I pay myself as the money comes in."

"Are you attached to doing it this way rather than, say, paying yourself each time we complete a group?"

Suddenly the storm clouds that had obscured Roger's vision cleared as if they had been sent scuttling off by a stiff breeze. Instantaneously, just by becoming aware of what he had hidden from himself, our friend got 'smart' again.

"Oh my gosh, I didn't see that. I didn't want to give up my 6%. I didn't want to have to wait to get my money until you finished each course; I wanted to use it as it came in. Wow! My investment in immediately taking my 6%, made it impossible to hear you. I actually blocked the sense of what you were saying because it threatened my agenda."

"Your hidden agenda," Shya prompted, "you had even hidden this agenda from yourself."

"Boy is that ever true. Thanks. Of course your idea of an escrow account makes sense."

That evening, as I saw Roger so eloquently explain to a room full of friends, acquaintances and strangers, about discovering his 6%, I realized that Roger's way of being, his whole bearing and demeanor were not just signs of maturing. Plenty of people age without letting go of the old behavior patterns that are a vestige of their childhood. No, Roger had truly transformed. I was happy for him. Shya put his arm around me and we leaned back to hear the rest of Roger's story.

I have heard a Yiddish term, 'kvell'. When I think of this word, I think of it as meaning to revel deeply in the richness of something and to really relish the moment. As Roger spoke, both Shya and I were kvelling. We knew that Roger was handing these people the keys to be stars and to be transformed themselves. Unabashedly, Roger recreated who he had been so long ago in a way that it became real again in the retelling. As he allowed a room full of folks to laugh with him about his 6%, his investment in his hidden agenda, he was demonstrating the possibility that they didn't have to judge themselves and that in fact it was possible to not only look at but laugh at their petty investments, their own 6%.

47

RECOGNIZING
HIDDEN AGENDAS

THERE ARE AGENDAS THAT PEOPLE ARE AWARE OF AND THEN there are those of which they are unaware. As we saw with Roger, it is the latter that causes the mischief that shows up in our ability to relate. In this chapter, we are going to identify some of the typical types of hidden agendas that the two of us have seen during the course of working with individuals who are looking for a mate, as well as with couples who are looking at the mechanics of their relationship. It has been our experience that when people see what they have been doing mechanically and don't judge what they see, they have a choice to continue their actions or not. Again, awareness allows for freedom from the domination of old behaviors. The simple recognition of unaware patterns, if not resisted but seen for what they are, will free you from the mechanical restraints of these previously unrecognized hidden agendas.

Before we look at the types of agendas that can interfere with a person's ability to relate, let's examine the mechanics of these strategies for living.

HOW AGENDAS WORK

People can only see what they already know. What they have no knowledge of does not exist. Minds act very much like computer programs. They function by comparison to the data that is already in the system. Therefore, anything that occurs outside of the program is not recognizable.

Back in the late '80s, when the two of us bought our first computer, we also set up our first database. In other words, we bought a program that we could use to keep track of the names, addresses and phone numbers of people wishing to be on our mailing list. The particular system we purchased would translate any data entered into a pre-set form. For instance, we could type in the words "ariel & shya kane" and our program would automatically convert it so that the first letter of each word would be capitalized to read "Ariel & Shya Kane". Further, the area where the zip code was entered would only take five numbers.

50

The problem was that this formula, while mostly accurate, didn't always work. There were times when an individual's last name was not capitalized, such as the name "den Ouden". Zip codes longer than five digits couldn't be entered and foreign zip codes, which included letters, were rejected also. Because this was an early database program and was less sophisticated than the ones we have today, there was no way to override the automatic pre-set fields. Obviously, the person who wrote this program could not conceive of all the uses for his creation. He was limited by what he knew to be possible and by what he had thought to create. So the program did not take into account that users might have European clients, that not all names are capitalized and that, in the future, zip codes would have more than five numbers.

Agendas act like those automatic fields. They were pre-set when we, as individuals, were much less sophisticated and they run without the benefit of what we have learned since their inception. Bringing awareness to our automatic programs acts like a complimentary software upgrade. It allows you to keep what works and modify what doesn't. This leads to appropriate behavior rather than having to repeatedly make mistakes, which you are powerless to correct.

CREATING A CONTEXT IN WHICH
TO SEE NEW POSSIBILITIES

If you are not aware that something exists, it may still exist in reality, but in your experience it does not. For example, in 1992 the two of us were in Hawaii with Max, Shya's 85-year-old father. We stayed at an ocean front condominium. From our vantage point, we could see migrating humpback whales spouting and jumping out of the water but Max could not. Then we took him out on a whale-watching trip where these enormous creatures came close to the boat. When we went back to the condo, he looked out at the ocean, and suddenly he could see the whales. Now he knew what to look for. We had pointed them out before the boat ride but he could not see them.

There has to be a context created in which to see. People look through what they already know and not unlike our early database program reject what isn't in their pre-set field of knowledge. So if they don't realize there is a whole other paradigm, a whole other reality, a whole other context in which to operate, for them it doesn't exist. You might think, *What is wrong with that?* The answer is nothing. However, what you know limits what is possible for you. There is a saying, "If you can dream it, you can have it". But, if you don't know the existence of something, you can't even dream it. Ask yourself, *What if there are things I don't know that could radically alter the quality of my relationships?*

Some of the limitations in your capacity for having an exciting, vital relationship are your unaware agendas or goals. (Webster's primary definition of agenda is "a program of things to be done.") On one hand, agendas and goals are very useful. They allow us to focus on those things that need to be completed. They allow us to steer a course to a destination. They keep us on track so that we don't get distracted and they allow us to see if we have achieved what we set out to accomplish. But agendas can also limit what we can see, fettering our interactions with others and with our environment. They do this because we are driven toward the completion of that goal and we become blinded, as Roger did, in our attempt to get what we think we want or need.

Take for example, a couple that is expressing their particular points of view about how to raise their children. One would assume that, since these people are working to have the best for their family, they would be working as a team to discover what is best for their kids. However, each comes in with a set agenda. The atmosphere is often competitive and adversarial. The outcome of the conversation often times is defined by whose agenda 'won' and whose 'lost'. In addition, if each individual's underlying hidden agendas are to not appear stupid or not let a man/woman tell them what to do, then the playing field is littered with hazards to a well-balanced resolution. It is as if each person's hidden agenda dictates the outcome. Rarely is it harmonious.

Another type of hidden agenda is when one or the other of the participants in a relationship feels that they must have an 'equal' say or they want to control the way the relationship functions. So he or she keeps score. For instance a woman might complain to herself, *Last time we went out, he decided which movie we were going to, so tonight, we better go see the movie I want or else!* Now, she may not be aware that she keeps score. The agenda to be in control and have the final say keeps score. She just feels that now it is her turn to say what movie they are going to.

We have a friend who grew up resenting that her parents seemed to favor her brothers. She grew up certain that men got special treatment and was out to prove not only her equality, but also her superiority. Our friend told us that, when she chose men to date, she had the agenda to pick men who were "less educationally pedigreed" and her whole approach was adversarial. If her partner seemed more intelligent than she, she would express her insecurities by picking a fight. Her whole strategy for a successful relationship, prior to bringing awareness to her way of relating, was to intimidate and dominate. It didn't allow for much in the way of intimacy. Her life choices were controlled by her unaware resistance to how her parents related to the boys vs. the girls in her family.

When you are operating through an unaware agenda, you do not listen to what is being said. When you have an idea or plan about the way a thing is supposed to go, you only see the relevance of what is being said as it applies to your agenda. True listening is a function of intentionally recreating the point of view of another. If you are operating through an agenda, you cannot possibly see another's point of view. You can only see it in relationship, in agreement or disagreement, to your preferences.

HOPE

Often agendas blind you to the truth of a situation because, as it was with Roger's 6%, you have a strong preference for life to show up the way you want it. Here is an example:

Julie's husband told her, "I need to get my own place for awhile. It is not personal to you or the kids, but I need to be alone and think about my life. I love you and don't want to be with anyone else, it's not about that. I just need some breathing room."

Although this was very difficult for Julie, she supported him in his move. This is not to say that fights did not erupt but, all things considered, it went smoothly. The couple kept things relatively friendly, at first, and continued to be sexually intimate. It was hard for Julie to see him get a lease for his new place and furnish it, complete with rooms for their children to spend the night. But through it all, he insisted that it wasn't necessarily permanent. "Just give me time," he would say, "If you are upset all of the time you will turn the kids against me."

Julie waged a battle within herself to stay centered. In her heart she loved him and dreamed that things would return to the way they had been, as she remembered them, from the early days of their relationship. And the sex was all the more intense because it wasn't so frequent and she really wanted to be with him when she could.

Each time Julie went for an interlude at her estranged husband's house, it was more and more like a home. First the carpets, then the curtains, then the small touches that he had not wanted to be a part of when they had created a home together. One day, while in his bathroom, Julie noticed condoms in his medicine cabinet. She confronted him. "Why do you have condoms? We certainly don't need them!" Julie knew full well that her husband had a vasectomy after the birth of their second child.

"It is not my *intention* to have sex with anyone else. I have condoms *in case* something were to happen. You know how important it is to have safe sex in this day and age. I honestly don't plan to be with anyone else. Why can't you believe me?"

Julie did not want to see the truth of the situation. She really wanted to believe he was sincere. Another word for Julie's agenda to have her husband back is: Hope. She desperately hoped that he would come home and this acted like a drug, dulling her senses to the reality of the situation.

Haven't you from time to time made choices where, in retrospect, you said to yourself, *What was I thinking?* PT Barnum once said, "You can't fool an honest man." Well, you can't fool an honest woman either. Julie's unexamined hopes and dreams kept her from being honest with herself about the reality of her situation.

DON'T TELL ME WHAT TO DO

Unaware agendas keep you from being appropriate with your life and may be conflicting and simultaneous. Here is another example: Drew is a handsome entrepreneur who is dating and looking for a relationship. But Drew, as a young child, defined himself by not wanting to be told what to do. Even now, if his mother, father or friend made a suggestion or request, he routinely did the opposite. In some ways, this behavior may actually have helped to strengthen his stamina to get things done. Drew surprised his family and friends by persevering in the face of terrible odds but it never occurred to Drew that many of the challenges he faced were of his own making.

One Friday evening, Drew had a date with a lovely lady in whom he was very interested. He was supposed to leave at 7:00, in time to pick her up for dinner and a movie. But, he didn't begin to get ready to leave until 6:30, which is not enough time to shower, shave, put on clothes and get out the door to be at her house on time. It is not as if he was busy all day. Instead, he goofed around, whittling away the hours until he was so pressed that he could only make it on time if there were absolutely no unexpected events, such as a phone call he needed to handle or traffic on the way. Drew, unbeknownst to himself, is so locked into his agenda of not being told what to do that he didn't even want to be told what to do by himself. This dynamic is commonly labeled procrastination. He set up the date but then resisted the time constraint because anything that tells him where to go and what to do, even his own schedule, is an anathema.

How many times do we as individuals operate like Drew? We want to have a magical relationship and yet, mystifyingly, our actions seem to be directly opposed to what we say we want.

Let's tease the Drew scenario out a little further. It is now 6:45 and Drew is rushing to leave. He showers, dumps his clothes in a heap, hastily shaves and rifles through his closet in search of the perfect outfit, discarding this and that until he finds something to wear. Now, leaving a trail of destruction behind him, he rushes back into the bathroom, combs his hair and automatically reaches for his cologne, spraying it liberally. Drew now freezes mid-spritz. He has just remembered that the woman he is going to meet has a severe allergy to scents of any kind. He now is pressured by the time and has to make a decision. *Oh well,* he thinks, *it will probably wear off by the time I get there, I can't be late,* and he rushes out the door.

Poor Drew. His date is now the recipe for disaster. He really, truly likes this woman. He also cares about her but his unwillingness to be told what to do, which he is unaware of, takes precedence over his adult aim of having a satisfying relationship. His resistance to being told what to do is the background, mostly unnoticed, upon which he plays his life. His reaching for that bottle of cologne and his dashing out the door anyway even after he realizes his mistake, acts out his resistance to having his life constrained by this other person's allergies. Somewhere, he resented being 'told' not to wear perfume. He is habituated to automatically challenging anything that seems to impinge upon his rights.

You might think that Drew's story is an extreme case. Not so. Here are more everyday examples:

The two of us were invited to a dinner where some of the guests were vegetarians and the host was not. He prepared baked red peppers, some of which he filled with beef and the others he stuffed with mixed vegetables. But somehow, raw ground beef just 'happened' to be in the final vegetarian dinner. Upon looking at this 'mistake' our host realized that his disagreement with his guests' food preferences was unawaredly displayed in his finished product.

A waitress told us that she had a tendency to forget orders or make mistakes when she disagreed with or didn't like the customer's food choice. She surprised herself by seeing that her agenda to be right about her taste in foods was more important than good service, customer satisfaction and tips.

We have seen one partner in a couple resist the other's way of doing things even though it destroyed the relationship. We have also seen people fired from jobs because they refused to follow how the boss wanted things filed or presented because the employee had to do things his or her own way, even if it cost them their livelihood.

THE TERRIBLE TWOS

Take a look at any two-year-old. A parent's admonition not
to touch something is the same as a command to touch it.
Sometimes this age is called the 'terrible twos'. This is because
at this age, children are virtually uncontrollable and have a
tendency to do everything that is contrary to what is being
requested of them. "No!" a child will emphatically state as he or
she rushes toward the street and the parent, aware of danger, has
to restrain him or her. Haven't we as adults seen how we have
behaviors that seem to be at war with what we are trying to
accomplish in our relationships? Hasn't the voice of reason
whispered *I better get ready to go if I want to be on time* and the other
voice in our heads wheedles and whines, *Just five more minutes,*
until we are so pressured that we can hardly make it on time?
That 'just five more minutes' conversation may sound suspiciously
like the one you had with your parents when they were trying to
get you to go to bed.

Drew has tried to analyze why he is often late to important
engagements. He has even made resolutions to be on time. So,
when faced with calling and communicating to his date and
giving her the option to say, "Don't worry about the cologne," or,

"Take a shower and come later," or, "Let's have our date another day," he rushes out the door in hopes of it being all right but, in all honesty, knowing that he is bringing a problem with him.

"How to fix this?" you might ask. Well, fixing or changing this pattern will lead to more inappropriate actions. Don't forget, Drew's resolution to be on time, as if this is the source of his problems, has blinded him to the fact that on time is not always the right or the only choice. If, on the other hand, you become aware of your hidden agendas, you will not have to act them out mechanically. With awareness you become free to make appropriate choices in your life.

INHERITED TRAITS

Some of your 'agendas' may actually be inherited traits. We, as individuals, may think we are making personal choices in our lives and be totally unaware that we are actually acting out some familial script that has been handed down, via our family lines, as a blueprint for survival. We know a fellow who breeds Peruvian Paso horses. They are known for their smooth gait and good temperament. We've been told that these traits have been reinforced through generations of breeding. This is true of humans also. Your family has learned to survive via some patterns of behavior, which are useful, but only if you do not have to operate through them or rebel against them.

Friends of ours, Jed and Lena, had a child, Anna, a beautiful, innocent baby, growing, absorbing and learning from her environment. We have known her parents for more than 15 years and during this time we have also seen them grow. We have seen their triumphs and their disappointments. Their life experiences have included births in the family and the death of loved ones. Lena has a particular facial expression when she is upset and crying. Her chin quivers, her lower lip sticks out of its own accord and these traits make her sadness or upset an endearing, sympathetic picture. When Lena cries, one is compelled to take notice and be sensitive and caring. Well, guess what? The day she was born, Anna, who had never seen her mother cry, had a miniature version of the quivering chin and protruding lip. She didn't 'learn' this behavior from her mother. It was a pre-set survival tool that she has in her infant's genetic toolbox of survival techniques.

TINY TEARS

Crying for an infant is a way of communication but as an adult in a relationship, it can be an annoying habit that individuals use in an attempt to avoid conflict. We have seen both men and women cry in an instant as a way to gain sympathy.

There once was a doll called 'Tiny Tears'. It was a favorite of young girls who got to practice being mommies and comforting the baby when it cried. We had a young client, Tina, who cried whenever she was on the spot. At work, the crying mechanism would turn on if she thought she was going to be given input by her boss. With her boyfriend, it was hard to have a serious conversation without the tears turning on. Her crying was as mechanical as Tiny Tears. If the circumstances applied a little pressure, her eyes would well up, whether she wanted them to or not. And Tina hated the crying. She was embarrassed at work and at home. It was a case of the three principles all over again. The more she tried to avoid crying, the more she was provoked to cry. As Tina began to let herself be teary without judging herself for it, the tears began to be less automatic. Tina also took one other important step. She told the truth that sometimes they were still a useful tool to gain sympathy. When she was young, crying was a ploy that kept her parents from punishing her. It was hard to be strict with someone who was already punishing herself so harshly. Crying her way out of difficult situations had become a way of life. The problem was that this way of relating did not support a functional relationship with her boyfriend nor support her advancing in her job and having a sense of well-being in her life. With awareness and the courage to tell the truth, the tears became a thing of the past.

65

WHAT IS LOVE?

There was a couple, Becky and Jake. When they were married, Becky continued with one of Jake's family traditions by making chicken soup every Friday evening. However, try as she might, Jake would always say, "Becky, your soup is very good, but it is not as good as my mother's."

So Becky bought the best ingredients, changed the spices, tried with more vegetables and still, "Thank you for making me this soup, if only it were as good as my mother used to make."

One Friday afternoon, Becky went down to the basement to take the clothes out of the washer and put them into the dryer when she discovered that the washing machine had overflowed and there was a tide of sudsy water covering the floor. By the time Becky got the mess cleaned up and returned back upstairs, she realized that the soup was burnt.

Frantic, because it was too late to get another chicken and start over, Becky set the table, decided to serve the soup anyway and hope for the best. When Jake got home and sat down to eat, she placed a bowl in front of him and returned to the kitchen for bread.

"Becky, get in here!" Jake bellowed. Cringing she apologetically returned. "Becky, this soup...finally, it's just like my mother's!"

When you are looking for a loving partner, you may automatically have a hidden agenda to look for the things you experienced as a child that you associated with love, even if they are not necessarily things that you would want in a partner from an adult perspective.

Like with the chicken soup analogy, you may pick a partner with the same attributes that you saw in your first love, your mother or father. If so, you will look for a man or a woman to relate with who embodies those old familiar ways of being or relating even if, in truth, they are not something you as an adult would prefer.

A child's mind is not discerning. Love from a parent can come with extras attached, such as anger, frustration, etc. Without awareness you may unwittingly be repeating a family tradition rather than choosing a partner who truly fits. If you grew up in a family that argues, you will look for a partner who will fight with you because that is your schematic for love.

With awareness, you can reveal those things that have been hidden and, if you do not judge yourself for being attracted to people with 'bad' attributes, the way will be open to build a partnership with your current mate or with a new partner that is one that will satisfy your adult desires for relationship rather than fulfill your child's idea of love.

E X E R C I S E S

RECOGNIZING HIDDEN AGENDAS

1. Notice if after reading this chapter you have inadvertently given yourself the new hidden agenda to be 'agenda-less'.

2. Notice when speaking with your partner if you have the agenda to be right about your point of view.

DON'T TELL ME WHAT TO DO!

ONE OF THE MOST BASIC INHIBITORS IN A LOVE RELATIONSHIP IS the resistance to being told what to do. People are afraid they may be dominated by their partner's desires and somehow forced to go along with, or do things, that are not what they really want. On the surface, this is a reasonable concern. No one wants to act as a 'doormat' or lose his or her independence. However, it never occurs to most people that even resisting simple requests is a basic behavior pattern that started at an early age. Have you ever watched a very young child throw a spoon or something off his or her highchair, over and over? Even if the parent says "don't", this action is like a very fun game to the child. When the child becomes mobile, he or she continues the game by running in the opposite direction from the parent. Saying "come here" is tantamount to a command to run somewhere, anywhere else.

Avoiding being told what to do is so normal that it has followed most of us through the many stages of our lives largely unnoticed. In the next section, as told from Ariel's point of view, she relates her experience about first noticing Shya and how his way of being was so different that it set him apart. In this story, you can see how mental processes follow us from an early age and how they become so normal that they are transparent. Perhaps it will take you back to times when you constructed the groundwork for your relationships, as you know them today.

In 1980, I took my first personal growth course. Taking this workshop was really exciting for me. I looked at how I related to my parents, my sisters and my life. I looked at my fears and aspirations, my career and appearance. I really went for it with everything I could muster. I remember we had to fill out a form and one of the questions was, "What do you want to get out of this seminar?" I was in heaven. This question was an easy one. I wanted to get work as an actress, lose weight, like myself better, improve my love life, stop being so afraid, fix up my relationship with Mom and Dad and about one hundred and ten other things. I even had to attach an extra sheet of paper to handle all of the items that needed work.

As it turned out, something freed up for me in that group. I went to three auditions the week following its completion and I landed all three parts. I was on a roll. But, by the time I went to the evening seminar where Shya walked into my life, the freshness and sense of freedom had already faded and I was an old pro at this new system I had just learned. Already my excitement for life had redimmed and I had replaced it with a reasonable facsimile of true enthusiasm.

"It's time for announcements," said Shya, our new seminar leader, from the front of the room. This was the third evening of a ten session series and this was the third time we had a new facilitator. Unbeknownst to me, these courses rarely had more than one leader but for some reason, we were on our third.

Announcements! We all knew what that meant and I was ready to show it. I sat up in my chair and along with the 200 or so others, I clapped and cheered and stomped my feet. This was the time when they offered other courses and projects and tickets to go to big groups with your friends at places like New York's Beekman Theater. We were all enthused.

"Oh, be quiet. I know all about you guys," Shya said as he settled into the chair in the front of the room. "You all clap and carry on, but you don't buy tickets or do anything. It's just for show."

Glancing down, I noticed my hands were suspended in mid-clap. Quickly I lowered them into my lap and looked back up at Shya. He was sitting quietly, just waiting. *He is the most arrogant person I have ever seen,* I thought. *Who does he think he is?*

"Listen, if you want to buy tickets, then buy tickets. If you don't, then don't. But making all of that noise is just insulting if you don't really mean it. If you want to buy tickets, then do it for you, not for my approval or anyone else's, for that matter. It's time to get honest about what you want."

The truth reverberated through the room. It was quiet. It wasn't forceful. Shaken from a mechanical complacency, suddenly I started to come alive again. The next thing I knew, my legs were taking me to the ticket table where I bought five. I didn't know to whom I would give them, but I wanted to buy them because

I wanted to, not because it was the right or expected thing to do. *Who does he think he is?* was replaced with, *Who is this guy?*

A year or so later, as I sat behind my receptionist's desk at Meltzer Chiropractic office, I looked up to see Shya filling out a form of his own. It was the new patient questionnaire. This gave me time to examine him up close. *This guy is quite handsome,* I thought as I inspected his short brownish hair, his lean physique and I must admit the rolled up sleeves of his dress shirt revealed a nice pair of forearms. And then, there was the motorcycle. Shya had arrived wearing a brown herringbone patterned sports jacket, shirt, tie and helmet. The biker look mixed with the corporate image I definitely found enticing.

When Shya left after that initial appointment, my real detective work began. As the door closed behind him, I took my cup of coffee and his chart and did a little research. In Shya's particular case, the new patient information form provided both the doctor and me with pertinent facts. I fully planned on reading the questionnaire with entirely different motives than Dr. Don had intended. I wanted to see if Shya was a good candidate for dating and so I scanned the form. *Hmm...41 years old. OK, I can live with that but what about...Great! He's single...no communicable diseases, heart problems, etc., etc. Excellent!*

When it came to the part on the back of the form where it said "Reason For Visit", I was pleased to note that Shya had filled in, in a strong distinctive handwriting, "For tight muscles and to relieve stress." *Oh good, he's not sick; he's just looking to take care of himself.*

I was happy that Shya's diagnosis called for him to come to the office three times a week for a series of weeks and then a number of weeks for two times and so on. He soon became one of the first patients on Mondays, Wednesdays and Fridays and eventually he came early enough to chat, share coffee and sometimes muffins.

One particular Friday morning started out normally enough but something happened that has highlighted that day in my memory and kept it from fading into the shadowy indistinction of past day-to-day events.

The outer door opened on a very gray day, the rain falling in sheets. As I buzzed Shya into the office, I watched as the heavy drops rolled off his face and down the khaki colored rain slicker. This day was definitely not the best for motorcycles or their riders. Shedding his outer wet layer, Shya held up the soggy paper bag that held our coffees. This had become a morning ritual. By the time he arrived, I was ready for a second cup and a break. I had begun looking forward to his visits.

That morning Shya's face and hands were particularly rosy from the cold and he held the steaming container of coffee in his cupped hands to soak up some of the warmth. This did nothing to heat his nose or the backs of his hands and so, teasingly, he touched his chilly fingers to my face. Squealing, I jumped back, a few drops from my cup sloshing over the side and onto my desk. Pulling a tissue to wipe up the spill I teasingly said, "Oh go away, you. Just be quiet; put your coffee down; take your chart and go into room 3. Lay down and wait for the doctor."

An amazing thing happened. Shya set his cup on the counter, and without saying another word, he picked up his chart, turned and went down the hall, turning the corner and moving out of my line of sight as he made his way to room 3. The reception area now became very still. The coffee steamed on the counter. The rain could be heard pelting down against the window and the goose bumps on my arm had nothing to do with the storm raging outside or the remembrance of chilly fingers on my face.

After a few moments, tossing the tissue in the wicker garbage basket, I quietly followed Shya down the hall and turned the corner so I could look into room 3. There his chart was, nestled in the Plexiglas door pocket waiting for the doctor so he could know at a glance whom he was seeing and review the course of treatment. It was surprising to me how often I had to chase after patients with their chart and slip it in the door for them, even though this should have become routine after the first couple of visits or so. And, there also was Shya, lying face down on the chiropractic table, relaxing and waiting for his turn with Dr. Don.

What a curious feeling. I hadn't realized, before that moment, how much people embellished upon or resisted even simple instructions. I couldn't remember people ever simply doing what they were told.

I rarely did what I was told, at least not exactly. One time, in fifth grade, I came in from recess one bright sunny spring day, only to be greeted by a lengthy test, which my teacher, Miss Tyler, had devised.

"OK, class," she said. "This is a math test. It is mainly

story problems..."

I hated her. It was unfair. Life was unfair.

"...You will have 60 minutes to finish the test. This exam will count very heavily toward your overall grade. There will be absolutely no talking. Anyone who talks or is found cheating will get an automatic 'F'. Those of you who finish early may go outside."

Fat chance. It was cruel of her, in my opinion, to entice us with the great outdoors because everyone knew that story problems were the bane of all math tests and now we had several pages to wade through in only one hour.

Miss Tyler faced the blackboard, picked up the chalk and in her best cursive script she wrote, "Be sure to read all of the instructions thoroughly before beginning. You will have 60 minutes." Then, chalk in hand, she pointed to each word and, as if we were morons, she also read them out loud, underlining the word all. Then she looked at the class and smiled. She actually smiled as she said, "Any questions?"

"OK children," she announced glancing at the clock, "Pick up your pencils, turn over your papers, read the instructions and begin."

Quickly I flipped the test over and I began. First the instructions: "Be sure to write clearly and legibly"...blah, blah, blah. I quickly scanned the pages to see if I could find a strategy that would let me finish the whole thing with a minimum of mistakes and still have a few minutes outside. As if to tease me, the breeze gusted and brought with it all of the fragrant promises of spring. Tightening my resolve, I sat up straight and dove into the pile of questions starting with number one.

I was diligently working through the fifth problem when Anita, the class smarty, put down her pencil, gathered up her test, handed it to Miss Tyler and went outside. I couldn't believe it. Next John got up and looking a bit smug, he handed the test in and went to play. One by one, students began finishing their tests. My friend, Jan, looked at me with a slightly sheepish grin as she headed out to the playground. I tried not to let it distract me. I was determined to get outside. Around about this time, Miss Tyler started chuckling and she was joined by the chuckles of Mr. Miller, the other fifth grade teacher who for some reason had appeared in front of our room. I found the combined laughter of the two teachers downright disturbing.

"Sshhh!" I found myself saying. I didn't think I would be risking an 'F' for reminding my teachers that we were working here and besides "Sshhh!" wasn't exactly talking.

My testy shush and glowering look didn't quite get the response I had expected. Miss Tyler and Mr. Miller suddenly broke into a fit. They laughed so hard that she began to hold her sides and exclaim "Oh, Oh, Oh!" as she tried to keep her sides from aching. We all stopped to stare as they snorted and wiped tears from their eyes.

"Ariel, did you read the instructions?" Mr. Miller asked while attempting to keep a straight face. Glancing around at the third of the class still seated, I protested as only a guilty child can, "Of course I did!"

Actually I hadn't really read the whole paragraph of instructions. I had wanted to get it over with. My noisy indignant protestations brought on a whole new wave of laughing and snorts and "Ohs!" and other odd exclamations from Miss Tyler and Mr. Miller.

"Class, please put down your pencils," Miss Tyler commanded and I was about to protest because we still had a half an hour left and I wanted to pass the test but something in her eye stopped me.

"Ariel, will you please read the instructions to the class."

In my best voice, trying to sound as if I actually had read them all, I began, "Be sure to write legibly and clearly. In the margins be sure to show your work. If you get the answer wrong, you will be awarded partial credit for work you did correctly. If you do not show how you arrived at your answers, you will not be credited even if you get the right answer. Be sure to read all of the questions before you begin. Answer only questions four, thirteen and thirty, hand in your paper without talking and then go outside."

"I can't see the rest of you wasting this beautiful day simply because you didn't follow my instructions," Miss Tyler said with a smile that seemed quite kindly now. "Go ahead and go outside with your friends," she continued as she dropped the tests she had collected into the waste paper basket, "And be sure to throw your tests into the trash before you go." This was one set of instructions I wasn't going to resist.

As I quietly returned to the reception desk of the chiropractic
office that day, I was as stunned as I had been that time in fifth
grade when I found out that I didn't follow the instructions.

Shya had simply done as he was requested. Why did I find this
so remarkable? I replayed my instructions in my mind:
*Oh, go away, you. Just be quiet; put your coffee down; take your chart
and go into room 3. Lie down and wait for the doctor.*

Shya hadn't taken that extra sip of coffee, nor had he said, "OK,"
or added any other filler, he had simply followed my instructions
and completely fulfilled my request. I am not sure why this
affected me so deeply, but it did. I was inspired by the economy
of his movements and touched that his actions seemed to be
without reservation. And I didn't feel like I had been bossing him
around either. He simply was responsive to my request and I felt
powerful, listened to and somehow special.

Once, Shya and I were walking down a street in New York City
when he suddenly stopped and whirled around, staring intently
at the retreating backs of a couple who had just passed us. "Rick,
is that you?"

The couple turned around. Rick was a fellow Shya had known while living in Maine, someone he had neither seen nor spoken with in almost 14 years. Rick, it turns out, was in Manhattan from his current home in Washington D.C., with his girlfriend, Lisa.

Shaking his hand, Lisa said, "Shya, I am glad to finally meet you. Rick has told me so much about you."

"In fact, I was just talking about you the other day to one of the CEOs I act as a consultant for. I was telling about the time you came to my house for a barbecue, do you remember it?"

When Shya shook his head, no, Rick continued, "It was the most amazing thing. I guess it happened about 18 or 20 years ago. You came to my house early one night when I was preparing dinner for our families and friends and you asked if there was anything you could help with. I told you that it would be helpful if you could clean the grill, chop a little firewood for later and bring the dishes out to the table. And you know what, you cleaned the grill, chopped a little firewood and brought the dishes out to the table. You didn't change the order in which you did these chores. You didn't add anything. You just did as I asked. It was almost as if there was a second 'me' out there doing those tasks and it was an amazing experience which I have never forgotten."

E X E R C I S E S

DON'T TELL ME WHAT TO DO

1. See if you can notice all of the ways you resist being told
    what to do, by yourself and by others.

SURRENDER VS. SUCCUMB

IT IS IMPORTANT TO ESTABLISH WHAT IS MEANT WHEN WE USE THE terms 'surrender' and 'succumb' and to distinguish between the two. There is a vast difference between surrendering and succumbing to the requests made upon you by your life and your partner. Surrender is when you take on another's request of you as though it were your own. Succumb is when you do what is requested of you and victimize yourself for having to do it.

How many times have you said, "Yes, I will," and then resented that you had to? This is succumbing. Succumb is when you complain in your thoughts about the injustice of the request and how you are only doing it because they asked it of you, but not because you want to.

We define surrender as allowing yourself to do what your life requests of you and sometimes, your life shows up as requests made by your partner. Surrender is when you fulfill a request as if it were your own idea in the first place, with the intention of having it be a really great idea. This is distinctly different from fulfilling the request with the intention to prove to your partner that he or she was mistaken or misguided to have asked in the first place. In other words, if you succumb to a request, you will not have fun and you will be proving him or her wrong. When you succumb, frequently you will hurt yourself somehow to show your partner just how wrong he or she is.

Many people find surrendering very challenging because once they are in a relationship, they start competing with their partners. This dynamic can be especially strong for women who compare themselves and their achievements and want to prove that they are equal to or as good as a man. It is also strong for men who have been programmed not to let 'girls' get ahead of them.

Many women have not discovered that they can just be themselves and still include their femininity. They haven't seen that they don't have to be manly in a man's world. They haven't recognized that they can be very potent and powerful as a human being, without force, because force looks really bad on a woman. Of course, it doesn't work so well for men either.

HERE IS WHAT TRUE INDEPENDENCE LOOKS LIKE:
THE ABILITY TO SURRENDER TO ANOTHER HUMAN BEING.
IF YOU DON'T HAVE THAT ABILITY TO SURRENDER TO
ANOTHER HUMAN BEING, YOU ARE NOT INDEPENDENT.
RATHER, YOU ARE TOTALLY RUN
BY A MECHANICAL WAY OF BEING,
"DON'T TELL ME WHAT TO DO!"

If you have the choice, the ability, the willingness, to surrender, then you are truly independent. It takes a very strong person to say, "Yes. . . yes. . .okay, yes. . .yes. . .sure. . .all right. . .yes."

If you have the ability to sidestep the early programming of not wanting to be told what to do by another, then you actually have the ability to honestly step forward and say, "No, I don't want to do that," when "No" is your truth. When you have the ability to surrender, you become powerful in yourself and your union with a partner becomes a powerful one. Whether your relationship is new or well seasoned, there is the possibility of surrendering to your life and your partner and having your relationships enter the realm of the miraculous.

COMPLETING YOUR RELATIONSHIP WITH YOUR PARENTS

BREAKING THE CYCLE OF UNFULFILLING RELATIONSHIPS

IF YOU WANT TO CREATE A WORKING, SUPPORTIVE RELATIONSHIP with another, it is imperative that you be willing to be complete in the relationship you have with your parents.

The dictionary defines 'complete' as: Lacking no component part; full; whole; entire.

What does being incomplete with your parents mean? It is when you are looking to prove them wrong or right for what they did, or didn't do, or when you endlessly search for their weak points. When you reference how you are living your life in comparison to how your parents have lived their lives and to what they did or didn't do for you, then you are incomplete. If, for example, in your opinion they were either there too much and smothered you or they were not there enough and you felt abandoned and misunderstood, these too, are symptoms of being incomplete. One way or the other, your source of identity is in relation and reaction to your parents. If you are saying that your parents are responsible for the way you relate then you are incomplete with them.

We have seen many adults who were children of highly successful people be failures in life and relationship because they wanted to prove to their parents that they did it wrong. Any time things started going too well, these people would sabotage the possibility of their own success. Being right was more important than being happy. The aversion to being like one's parent is non-discriminatory; you can't just pick and choose the parts of him or her you don't want to be like. If you are trying to not be like them you will avoid even their 'good' traits.

You can't be yourself if you are avoiding being like one or the other of your parents because then you are not living your own life. If you are resisting your parents, or going for their approval for that matter, then each action is filtered in a nanosecond through your idea of how they would do things rather than simply being yourself.

If you are still blaming your mother or father for the way you are, you will be handicapped in your ability to have a fully satisfying relationship. Your relationship to your parents is your archetypical relationship to men and women. They did not do it wrong. They were just living their lives as best they knew how and you happened to be born into that family. Your parents probably didn't take any courses on parenting or on how to have satisfying relationships. Neither did their parents...nor theirs. Until recently, probably the last 30 or 40 years, there have not been classes in parenting or relating. The way people are is the way they learned to be in the families in which they grew up. And, your parents did the best they knew how to do.

From a child's point of view, your parents should have done things differently. Children's perspectives are centered on themselves and on what they want. They cannot take into account all of the complexities of earning a living, having to relate with other people and being responsible for the well-being and survival of the family. Children, by definition, have an immature and limited perspective of reality and can only filter day-to-day events through how these events affect them and their desires, preferences and wants.

At a young age you, as a child, made decisions about who your parents were and then have held those decisions over time as though they are true. Most people don't realize that many of their opinions were formed when they were in a childish temper tantrum or contraction many years ago.

LE ANNE

Our friend, LeAnne, can now laugh at her child's interpretation of the things her father did 'wrong'. One rather dramatic childhood memory had to do with a vacation she had with her parents in Greece. While traveling about the country, they stopped at a scenic overlook. Because LeAnne was not tall enough to see over the stone wall that hugged the cliff face, her father lifted her up and stood her on top so that she could enjoy the view. LeAnne was scared by the height and through her immature perspective she made up the story that her father was trying to throw her over the cliff. This fable remained in place for years, repeated to herself and embellished over time. Eventually, LeAnne realized that she had made up a very imaginative, creative explanation to justify her fear and further saw that her father had no intention of doing her harm, nor desire to hurt her in any way. Bringing awareness to how she related to her father released her from her expectation that men were out to hurt her.

Some people reading this book will have had parents who, in fact, were abusive or severely lacking in parenting skills. We do not mean to suggest that some individuals did not experience severe childhood trauma. What we are suggesting is that carrying around a vendetta with one or both of your parents will severely hamper your ability to relate. Even if your parents did things that were insensitive, ill advised or abusive, there comes a point where you must choose between having a fully satisfying life or being right about how your parents did you wrong.

IF YOU WANT A RELATIONSHIP THAT WORKS,
THEN YOU MUST GIVE UP MAKING
YOUR PARENTS RESPONSIBLE FOR YOUR ACTIONS
AND START LIVING YOUR OWN LIFE.

You can either dwell in the events of the past, real or imagined, or you can include them and move on. Second principle: You can either be dedicated to reliving the past and trying to figure out, change or blame others for what happened, or you can live your life including but not dominated by those past events.

Here is an example, as told from Shya's point of view, where a young woman's vendetta with her father was so strong that it dominated her life and life choices. Nancy's personal war with her dad turned even a casual conversation into a battlefield.

A number of years ago we were invited to join a friend of ours, Jackie, and her friend, Nancy, for dinner. We showed up at the corner bistro and the four of us were seated at a table near the window. As soon as the waiter gave us a wine list and the menus, we engaged in the kind of small talk you have when you are meeting someone for the first time.

This dinner was in the era when New York City still allowed smoking in restaurants. Before the waiter returned to take our order, Nancy got out her pack of Marlboro's, a lighter and looking me in the eye she said, "Do you mind if I smoke?"

Although I don't smoke and don't particularly enjoy being in a smoke filled environment, I do my best not to impose my standards on others, so I said, "Go ahead, be my guest."

Nancy's response was quite shocking. Her face went white. She immediately raised her voice, "What do you mean you don't mind? You lead seminars, you are supposed to care about people!"

Ariel, Jackie and I all looked at each other. This outburst was so unexpected. I explained, "Listen Nancy, you are a grown woman. If you want to smoke who am I to tell you not to? It isn't about whether I care about you or not, it is your choice whether or not you smoke and none of my business."

Nancy leapt to her feet shouting, "How could you be so insensitive? I can't believe that you would be so uncaring and unfeeling that you would let me smoke in your presence without telling me it is bad for me. You are just like my father!"

And then, without saying another word, she grabbed her pocketbook and ran out into the night.

Jackie later told us that Nancy had never had a successful relationship with a man. Her incompletion with her father kept being superimposed over any man she met. Her vendetta with her dad had Nancy find fault with all men in her environment both casually and in potential romantic situations and this precluded any meaningful relationship with a man.

As human beings we have infinite possibilities. But, when your life is based on resisting or punishing your parents, there is only one possibility, and that is reenacting the dynamics you have created with them over and over with others. Therefore, your incompletion with one or the other of your parents eventually dictates your whole life strategy. It is ironic because it would seem that resisting them would give you independence, but what it actually does is tie you to them, forever.

MELANIE

Here is another example of how being incomplete with one or both of your parents will keep you from having a magical relationship and will also keep you from having a satisfying life:

Melanie kept moving from one boyfriend to the next and we suspected that she chose them less for love and more for the shock value they had with her family. She dated men of different ethnicity, religious groups, social backgrounds and tended to end the relationship when the people around her came to like and accept each new beau. At other times, she tended to find men who would beat or abuse her.

Interpersonal relationship was not the only area in which Melanie struggled. After many years of battling her way through college, she finally earned her Masters degree in Social Work. Knowing how difficult it had been for her to accomplish this, family and friends threw Melanie a party to honor this achievement. We attended this celebration and here is what happened:

Melanie came up to us, glass of champagne in hand and flatly stated, "Now I will get my Doctorate. Then my father will listen to me." And then she walked away. Poor Melanie. No achievement, no relationship, will ever be satisfying unless she discovers how to complete her relationship with her father.

ADULT SURVIVORS OF CHILDHOOD

A fellow came to see us who considered himself an adult. According to the story of his life, he had survived his painful childhood. But, his interpretation of the childhood he had survived came from the distortions and misrepresentations of a child's mind. Let's be specific:

David had spent many years seeing different therapists and psychiatrists examining his childhood as a way of explaining his adult failings, depressions and feelings of insufficiency, inadequacy and insecurity. Touch on any aspect of his life and he had a string of chronological events dating back to his childhood to explain why he was the way he was. And most of these explanations pointed to his father as the reason for all of his faults. The traumatic incidents on his list of his father's wrongdoings tripped off his tongue like a well-worn script. Everything that David considered a current failing was linked to this list and could be traced back to this familiar story.

When people are pre-occupied with their internal conversations about their childhood, they become paralyzed and ineffective. Their lives become a series of investigations into why they act the way they do and what caused them to be 'screwed up'. There is a pitfall in rehashing one's life. It is paradoxical: On one hand, it is laudable to investigate those things that seem to inhibit productivity and well-being. But on the other hand, this same investigation can keep you lost in looking to blame something or someone outside yourself for how your life is showing up. When this is the case, then you will keep going back to, *If I had a different family, then my life would be different,* or *If my parents didn't get a divorce then I wouldn't have trouble in relationships.*

There comes a point in each of our lives where there is an opportunity to actually take control. To take command of your life, it requires putting both hands on the steering wheel and going forward. If you are addicted to looking at your past to determine your future, it is as though you are driving down the road looking in the rear view mirror to figure out what turns are coming ahead. Then you wonder why your fenders are so dented by life. To take control, you have to let go of your past and be with what is, rather than blame it on the history that came before.

What we are suggesting is that there is a possibility outside of the psychological interpretation in which your life is determined by pivotal events that happened in your childhood. If one chooses to use a psychological model then those past pivotal moments determine one's life. This means that there is no possibility to ever recover from those events.

There is available to humanity, at this point in time, a paradigm shift from cause and effect to 'isness' — from a psychological paradigm where our lives are determined by events in our past to a transformational approach where things just are the way they are, not because of some prior event.

No two things can occupy the same space at the same time. You cannot be living your life directly if you are already preoccupied with figuring out why you are the way you are. You can either be actively engaged in your life or thinking about your life. You cannot do both simultaneously. If you are living your life directly, you discover the possibility of true satisfaction, well-being, a sense of security and capability. As a result, you stop worrying about whether or not you are doing it right, if other people would approve of you or even if you would approve of yourself.

IF YOU ARE LIVING YOUR LIFE DIRECTLY,
YOU NO LONGER WORRY ABOUT YOUR CHILDHOOD.
IN FACT, YOUR CHILDHOOD BECOMES
TOTALLY IRRELEVANT TO YOUR LIFE
AND YOUR ABILITY TO CREATE MAGICAL RELATIONSHIPS.

DON'T OFFEND YOURSELF

WE ONCE KNEW A 60 YEAR OLD WOMAN NAMED SUSAN WHO WAS very incomplete with her parents. According to her story, her deceased father had been an angry man. However, Susan particularly had incompletions with her mother, also deceased. These incompletions kept being replayed with all other women in her life including those younger than she, such as her own daughter-in-law, Megan.

Susan called us for an individual consulting session because she had a problem. It seems that, in her opinion, Megan was offensive and treated her with disrespect. Her biggest fear was that her daughter-in-law, who was pregnant and about to have her first child, would refuse to allow her to see the baby. According to

Susan, Megan was mean, vicious, nasty and vindictive. Wanting to fix the situation, Susan was desperately searching for a way to make Megan like her.

Having discovered that it takes two to fight and one to end the fight, we explained to Susan that our approach is based upon personal responsibility. We directed her to look at her part in the dynamics of their relationship that produced the disharmony between herself and her daughter-in-law.

Most of us don't look at our lives as though we are scientists. Usually when something happens that we don't like, we do not go back and investigate the precursors to that event. We don't look at what was said or done that led to the eventual trouble. So it appears to us as though the other person unreasonably got upset and we rarely look at our part in the matter of how that person responded to us. What did we do, or not do, that set them off?

What Susan hadn't looked at was the fact that she had strong judgments about Megan. She also hadn't seen that she was jealous about how her son was now paying more attention to his wife than he was to her. She was upset, annoyed and looking to find fault with Megan. During the course of the conversation it was revealed that Susan still harbored a grudge for how the couple had planned their wedding years ago. She continued to gather agreement from Megan's mother and others about how things should have been done differently. Susan had been applying pressure, sometimes silently and other times openly, to get the couple to live their lives according to her idea of what was right. It hadn't occurred to Susan that her attitude and interference in her son and daughter-in-law's lives might actually be the instigator of the stress in the relationship rather than it being a character flaw of Megan's.

Subsequently, we invited Susan to join us in one of our weekend workshops. It has been our observation that how one does anything is how one does everything. We felt that her participation would allow her to observe how she interacted with others, thereby gaining further insight into the dynamics of her relationship with her daughter-in-law. We must admit that we were surprised by how events unfolded over the course of that weekend seminar.

On Friday evening, everyone introduced themselves and people were genuinely excited to be there and meet each other. Susan fit right in. By Saturday afternoon, however, the dynamics of how she related to others and to her environment began to be revealed. In the afternoon session, we asked everyone how the lunch break went and a fellow named Alex spoke up. He reported in a very calm manner that he had gone for a meal with Susan and another person, neither of whom he had previously met. He stated that lunch with Susan felt strangely combative and he had started to feel very irritated with her. According to Alex, Susan's questions and comments before and during the meal were driven by her agenda to get what she wanted. He felt that she was pushy and only wanted things to go her way, not taking others into consideration at all. Alex actually chuckled at himself. He told us, and Susan, that in the past, before he knew the mechanics of how his mind worked, he would have started arguing and being belligerent just for the sake of taking the opposite position from hers. With awareness, he was able to sidestep the confrontation.

We thought that this feedback was extremely valuable to Susan because her self-perception was that of 'sweet old lady who wouldn't hurt a fly'. She was totally unaware that she had strong opinions for and against things, even seemingly insignificant topics, such as selecting a restaurant for lunch.

The next morning as people arrived we saw another interaction between Susan and another participant that was very telling. Helen arrived wearing her favorite straw hat, a recent gift from some close friends. As we stood nearby, we heard Susan comment softly, "Nice hat."

Helen was in the midst of putting down her bag and didn't hear the comment. She began to look inside her pocketbook for some gum saying, "Where are you? I know you are in here somewhere." Shortly, Helen found her pack of gum, popped a piece in her mouth and went to take her seat.

Later, Susan privately expressed to us her experience of what had happened, both with Alex and with Helen. First she said, "It really is too bad about that man with the anger problem."

"What man are you talking about?" we replied.

"Oh, that Alex. Obviously he is a very angry man. I never did anything at lunch to provoke him. And, Helen is very abusive also. In fact she practically ruined the workshop for me."

"What are you referring to, Susan?"

"Well, this morning I complimented her on her hat and she turned away from me in a huff and totally ignored me. Then she said under her breath, "I only wear this stupid *!#@$% hat because it is hot outside!"

We were dumbfounded. Having witnessed the interaction, Susan's conclusion could not have been further from the truth. She rewrote history to make her point of view right at the expense of her relationships with Alex and Helen. She was now harboring resentments against both of them for events that did not happen the way she remembered them. Susan had taken something that had, in fact, never happened and offended herself with it. The idea of personal responsibility was a foreign concept to her. Susan's experience was rewritten to reframe circumstances to fit her point of view. It now became apparent to us that Megan was very likely the scapegoat for Susan's misinterpretations of life.

YOU ARE NOT THE STORY
OF YOUR LIFE

EVERYBODY HAS A STORY

IF WE WERE TO ASK YOU WHERE YOU GREW UP, WENT TO SCHOOL or inquire about your favorite foods, you would be able to supply the answers in great detail. Your story contains the history of your life and relationships, highlighting those wonderful, positive experiences as well as the negative ones.

People define themselves by their stories. If you want to know what your story consists of, start to notice the labels or internal conversations that you have. Here are some examples of the ways in which you might categorize yourself:

I am: A Man/Woman

Single

An American

Not Good Enough

A Good Listener

From A Broken Home

An Alcoholic

A Mother/Father

Stupid

Divorced

Intelligent

A Teacher

Misunderstood

Christian/Jewish/Muslim

Not Good In Relationships

Too Fat

Of course, this is just a very limited list that we are using here as an example of some of the labels that people affix to themselves. If you look, you will find that there are many labels from your own experience that you can add.

THE LIMITATIONS OF LABELING YOURSELF

Your story is limiting. It defines what is possible for you in your life. Once in place, a story is self-sustaining. It gathers evidence to prove itself right. We once knew a lovely young woman, Fran, who had a story that she was not attractive and no one would want to date her. As a result, she was quite unaware that there were men who were interested. One afternoon at the local health club, we were sitting in the hot tub with Fran when a young man came and joined us. His interest was obvious. He asked her name, engaged her in conversation and he had little or no attention on anyone else. A short time later, after this fellow left, we commented that he seemed to be a sweet guy and it was nice that he was so attracted to her. Fran was dumbfounded. She hadn't noticed any of the nuances of the conversation or any of the blatant flirting for that matter. Her story acted like a set of blinders, filtering out what was obvious to anyone else.

A computer can only extrapolate from what it already knows, in other words, out of the information that is contained in it. It cannot conceive of anything outside of its known set of information. It is the same for the human mind. It is impossible to conceive of possibilities outside the known. In Fran's case, she could only imagine a possible relationship that conformed to her story of her life, which suggested that men would not be interested in her. Therefore, she completely filtered out those things that did not fit.

There is a principle in quantum physics that states that a sub-atomic particle can exist simultaneously everywhere in the universe. A particle has infinite possibilities of existence until it is measured. Once measured, however, it is forever defined by that measurement and that is its only possibility. Human beings also have infinite possibilities for their lives. But, as with sub-atomic particles, the moment you label yourself, you restrict your potential from limitless down to the narrow label by which you have defined yourself.

Let's take a moment to draw a distinction between the *fact* that you are a man or a woman, for example, and using the *label* of your gender as a primary source for your self-identification.

Shya is a man. He can either filter his life events through that perspective and use it as the reason things happen, or to justify his actions, *I am a man, therefore…* or, he can live his life as a human being who happens to be of the male gender. In the former, his gender dictates and determines his interpretation of his life experiences. In the latter, the individual that he is determines his life and he happens to be a man. The first allows no responsibility. The responsibility is blamed on the gender he was born: *Because I am a man, that is why people treat me the way they do.* The other allows for something called responsibility, the ability to respond appropriately to the events that occur in your life.

Here is another example of how taking a fact about your life and using it as a label limits you:

Colleen got divorced two years ago and the separation was painful. When she started to get her life back together, she joined a divorce support group that was comprised of men and women who were going through the divorce process. It was helpful to know that she wasn't alone in grieving and in her sense of confusion and anger at the dissolution of her marriage. However, the group also had a limitation that soon became apparent. Its dynamics were such that people who started to date and have fun were not well tolerated. There was an unstated commitment to being part of a group of 'divorcees'. As Colleen began dating, the group of friends and acquaintances she had made at this support group subtly, and not so subtly, discouraged her from moving on with her life. She found that as soon as her life included the fact that she had gotten a divorce, rather than being centered on it, she was no longer welcome in that group. She no longer fit the unspoken rules that she must be in pain, angry with her ex-husband and not enjoying the dating process.

LIVING BY THE RULES

You have a story about the way you are, but you also have one about the way things should be. You have a system of rules that dictate your behavior and many of them are unexamined. They were given to you, or made up by you, when you were young. This system includes what is proper behavior in relationships; how a man should be; how a woman should be, and if you blindly live by these rules, any relationship is doomed to fail.

If you pigeonhole yourself and use the rules of etiquette to determine your proper behavior, rather than looking and seeing what your truth is as an individual, then there is no possibility for true self-expression. The culturally imposed dictates of proper male or female behavior, or the resistance to those rules, run your life.

As you grew up, you got overlapping sets of rules and they conflict with each other. Here is an example:

The other day we got into an elevator and pressed the button for the lobby. Two floors down, a woman got into the car. She appeared to be an executive employed in the building. Before reaching the lobby, the car stopped again and a couple of men entered. When we arrived at the ground floor, the woman got irritated with the men for not stepping aside to let her exit first. If you were to ask her, she probably would tell you that she wants to be treated equally and that she doesn't like it when someone is condescending to her because she is a woman. But she also has unexamined rules of etiquette that conflict with her experience as an individual. This type of conflict can destroy the possibility of having a magical relationship. *I want to be an independent woman, but why didn't you open the door for me?*

These rules of etiquette, culturally derived from the past, may not be relevant or true for you as an individual. And if you apply them to relationships, you will always be inappropriate. To be appropriate, one must look and see what is true, in each moment, not apply a rule. When you get into the moment, you still have the story of your life but it loses its power over you.

A TRANSFORMATIONAL PERSPECTIVE

Reality is a function of agreement. In other words, if enough people agree that something is true, by agreement, it becomes the truth. Ultimately, it may not be accurate but for the moment, by virtue of popular opinion, it is. For instance, there was a time that everybody knew that the world was flat. It was the prevalent point of view and held to be the truth. In our world today there is the point of view that we are the result of our upbringing and our experiences and that these experiences have not only formed who we are, but also will determine what's possible for us in the future. From this point of view, our lives are predetermined by what has happened in our pasts. In effect the story of our lives, left unexamined, has ultimate power over us.

We would like to offer another possibility: A transformational point of view. From a transformational perspective, it is possible to notice that you have a story or an idea of who you are but you do not have to believe that this idea is the truth.

What if that story actually has nothing to do with how you live your life or how well you create relationships from this moment forward? This is what it will take. You will have to start looking to identify how much of the time that story is actually a complaint. You will need to see how your internal conversation complains about your life and justifies itself for complaining.

Here are some examples of how the conversation that you listen to and believe to be you might sound:

I am depressed because it is raining.

I don't really want a relationship, anyway.

My parents raised me wrong.

I am upset because my boyfriend left me.

I am better off alone.

I am not good at dating.

I am a mess because I came from a dysfunctional family.

I am not relationship material.

If you bring your awareness to the conversation you listen to, you will start to recognize certain patterns of thought that heretofore you believed to be true. Again, our definition of awareness is a non-judgmental seeing of what is. Awareness allows for recognition. Recognition leads to resolution. As you recognize thought patterns and do not make what you discover right or wrong (again awareness is a non-judgmental seeing) you will not have to believe or engage in these thoughts.

Letting go of your story will take courage, a lot of courage, because the story is familiar. It is like an old friend that has been there with you forever. The story is the known. But with courage, you can be your own Columbus, off to discover a whole new world.

WHEN YOU DISENGAGE FROM YOUR STORY,
YOU STILL HAVE THE FACTS OF YOUR PAST
BUT YOUR PAST EXPERIENCES NO LONGER DETERMINE
OR LIMIT WHAT IS POSSIBLE FOR YOU NOW.

Here is an example of how it works:

We have a friend, Sam, who has a terrific story. Sam was born with a severe hearing disability, 95% hearing loss in one ear and 75% in the other. He has worn hearing aids since he was an infant. Despite this condition, he was able to lead a relatively normal childhood. He attended a mainstream school; had friends; watched TV; played football and engaged in the activities you would expect from a 'normal' boy. So, up until the time Sam started 6th grade, all in all, it was just an OK story, but things were about to get radically more dramatic.

One fall day, when his stepfather came to wake him up for

school, Sam refused to get out of bed. Even as his stepfather got irritated, Sam wouldn't stop 'goofing around'. He just lay there.

It turned out that the day before, while playing a game of touch football with his pals, Sam had collided heads with another boy. While the bump didn't seem so important at the moment of impact, the result was that Sam didn't get out of bed that morning because, at the tender age of eleven, he had suffered a massive stroke that had paralyzed the entire right side of his body.

Sam had to learn everything all over again such as how to crawl, how to walk and how to talk. Before the stroke, he was right-handed so he had to learn how to do everything with his left. To this day, Sam has spastic paralysis in his right arm.

Pretty good story, right? Of course there is much more that happened as Sam moved through adolescence toward adulthood but you get the idea.

When we met our friend, he was defined by his story. It made him special, got him attention and was a compelling excuse for not having a relationship and a great life.

When we first met Sam, he was unkempt, unemployed and collecting disability. He was rude and if people reacted to his manner, he would think, *They are rejecting me because they are prejudiced against disabled people.* It never occurred to him that he was rejecting people first out of his own prejudice against himself.

Once Sam started to drop the labels by which he defined himself and brought awareness to his attitudes, actions and behaviors, he was able to look objectively and honestly at situations. He became more interested in other people, in having friends and being productive than in perpetuating his story.

Today, Sam is no longer a disabled man. He is happily married and is a successful furniture designer and craftsman. By the way, he still has that paralysis and hearing loss.

Sam used to hide behind his disabilities. With awareness, he discovered that he had something to do with how people interacted with him. Here is what he has to say about it:

"I was 28 when I finally met Marie, who is now my wife. Before that time, I only had one girlfriend, for a total of three weeks. I hardly ever dated. I told myself I couldn't date because

I was handicapped and girls wouldn't like me. In college there were lots of girls who were interested in me, I'll tell you that, but it didn't fit my story.

I just couldn't hear that people were interested in me and that wasn't because I am hard-of-hearing. It was because I was very attached to the story of being handicapped and disabled. Sometimes, a girl would give me her name and number but I wouldn't call her because I thought she was joking. It just didn't compute. I thought, *Who would want to date me?* I would come across girls' names and numbers on scraps of paper in my things but just couldn't put two and two together. I didn't call them. I kept my story.

The few dates I did have, I thought I had to tell my life story and that really turned the girls off. When I look back at that time, I wonder, *What was I thinking?*

When I started dating Marie, I don't really recall who initially asked the other out. At first, if we would have a disagreement about something, then the story would kick in, *This can't work because I am handicapped,* or *She won't really stay with me because I am disabled.* But now, after 10 years of marriage, it hardly comes up and then only for a moment. My story isn't really relevant anymore."

Sam's wife, Marie, is a beautiful and intelligent woman. Originally from France, she graduated from the Sorbonne in Paris, Summa Cum Laude in her Master's program. She teaches French and is an administrator in a private high school. Certainly, before Sam brought awareness to his way of relating, she would have been 'out of his league'. If Marie had shown interest, he would have thought that yet another woman was 'just joking'.

THERE ARE NO HAPPY VICTIMS

By definition, a victim is one who is abused in some way by another or by life's circumstances. Have you ever seen a happy victim? One of the prerequisites of being a victim is to be sad or demoralized or upset. Frequently, we victimize ourselves by listening to our own thoughts and believing that what we are telling ourselves is true. For instance, Sam told himself over and over that he was a victim because of his handicaps. As he started to bring awareness to his internal conversations and his behavior, those negative ways of relating started to dissolve.

The shift was instantaneous and it was progressive. As he was honest with himself about how inappropriate his behavior was toward others, those negative ways of relating stopped virtually over night. As he began to realize that the labels he had placed upon himself were limiting, he began to live his life rather than complain to himself about why he couldn't have one.

119

You might be reading this and saying, *"But you don't understand, I AM a victim. A horrible event has taken place in my life."* Perhaps this is true, but now what?

THE SUGGESTION HERE IS
NOT THAT UNFORTUNATE EVENTS DON'T HAPPEN,
BUT THAT HOW YOU
PROCEED IN THE FACE OF ADVERSITY
MAKES ALL OF THE DIFFERENCE
IN THE QUALITY OF YOUR LIFE.

Even if you came from a broken home or an abusive relationship, you can still create a magical relationship through awareness and living your life from this moment of now.

Remember Sam? We have yet to tell you another piece of his

personal history. Before he met us, a large part of his story was that he was a victim of sexual abuse. And he was. From the age of six to the age of sixteen, a man routinely, sexually abused him. In order for Sam to have the relationship he now has, he had to have the courage to stop using that abuse as a justification for not creating a magical relationship. He had to purposefully give up the idea that he was permanently damaged by those traumatic events in his childhood.

THE THREE PRINCIPLES OF TRANSFORMATION AND THE STORY OF YOUR LIFE

Let's revisit the three Principles of Transformation in relation to the story of your life. First: What you resist persists. Therefore, anything that you have resisted in your life story, such as your parents divorcing or your own failed relationships, will persist and tend to dominate your life. Next: No two things can occupy the same space at the same time. As with Sam, the more he listened to his story that no one would want to be with him, the more he gathered evidence to prove this point of view right. His pre-occupation with his story kept him from seeing what was right in front of him – available, interested women. The third principle is: Anything that you allow to be exactly as it is will complete itself and lose its power over your life. When Sam allowed himself to have his story without resisting it, judging it or believing it, he began to extract himself from his own unhappy tale.

You can either be right about your story or you can have a life and create the possibility of magical relationships.

E X E R C I S E S

YOU ARE NOT THE STORY OF YOUR LIFE

1. As you go about your day, notice the ways in which you categorize or label yourself.

2. Notice the rules you have for how to be in relationships.

3. Notice when you use the story of your life to justify your current actions.

Here is an example of what to look for:

We once met a man in his thirties who rarely made his bed. He claimed the reason was that his mother never showed him how.

THE ONE WHO LISTENS

THE STORY OF YOUR LIFE EXISTS IN YOUR MENTAL COMMENTARY about yourself and your life circumstances. Join us now as we return once again to the New York City Monday evening seminar as written from Ariel's point of view. Come explore with us and the other participants our transformational approach to creating magical relationships. It is also an opportunity to continue investigating the ways in which you categorize yourself.

Things in the room that Monday evening got quiet for a moment. Well, actually for more than a moment. Sometimes, when the topic we have been discussing comes to a natural conclusion, there is a gap. When this happens, the silence becomes deafening as people mentally scramble to figure out what to do or say next. Of course, this is the same gap that comes before most acts of creation or before engaging in something new and challenging. It is the time when the mind steps in and tells you all of its reasons why you aren't up to the task ahead or why you shouldn't take that risk. *You are too fat,* it whispers, *you might be rejected. You are too old,* or *too young,* it repeats insidiously. *Don't even try, you are unqualified. You might look stupid!* In our evening sessions, these quiet moments are the times when many have to wrestle with this private voice and the idea that what he or she has to say might be dumb, boring or insignificant. Folks are fearful that what they are worrying about, others might find unimportant or they are afraid of finding out something bad about themselves.

As we sat there that evening, our eyes averted to the floor so as not to add any heat to the group's already rising internal pressure, I was reminded of a film I used to check out from the school library when I was in fourth grade. The technology was a lot different back then. It was a lot less sophisticated than what is available now, but when I was nine, it was exciting nonetheless.

In a dark alcove of the basement library at West Gresham Grade School, I would sit watching the small viewing screen on many a morning. I suppose there were many subjects captured on tape for us to watch but there was one particular short subject that piqued my imagination. Filmed with the aid of time-lapse photography, a plant sprouted, grew, budded out and finally blossomed into a glorious red rose, glistening with dew. What a fascinating sequence!

In this system the tape ran like a loop. Once the rose had fully blossomed, the viewer was suddenly back at the beginning as the tape started over. Since it was spliced together to form a loop, there was no rewinding. It just played as a continuous miniature movie and I watched it again and again.

It wasn't just that technology was less sophisticated back then, so was I. On several successive trips to the library, I did my own personal science experiment with that brilliant red rose: I watched that tape many, many times, hoping, waiting and looking for it to change. I studied it intently to see if I could see a difference in the flower as it grew. I wanted to know if the leaf on the left would unfurl itself first or if, perhaps, the blossom would be a paler shade of red. Over and over I watched that tape loop. Somehow, I hadn't put it together that it was pre-set, pre-taped and that the end was linked to the beginning so that there was no chance of its changing. I guess I didn't grasp the concept that this loop was already completed, finished in the past by some other person, at some other time, in some other place. That tape of the rose was so fascinating, I wanted to believe it was currently alive and I fervently wished to see it change.

As Shya and I sat waiting for the next brave soul to speak, I knew from experience that many in the room were facing their own private tape loops. These compelling mental recordings are available for viewing whenever we are about to embark on something challenging that requires a leap into the unknown. This is the time when the tape will play the private *don't make a fool of yourself* message or it will resurrect some old, embarrassing event from school. Not having caught on that those tapes remain the same, most folks are waiting for the loop to change before giving themselves permission to go for their lives with passion. In many instances, I have seen individuals disappointed in themselves because they thought they had progressed beyond such old limited ideas and negative thoughts. They haven't grasped the concept that these thought loops were already completed, finished in the past by a younger version of themselves, at some other time, in some other place. As we sat there, I could feel people listen to an old story of themselves as if it were a current event.

I stole a peek at those sitting there, and I knew many didn't know they were watching a video and listening to a series of recordings. For a lot of folks, there is no distinction between the voice they listen to and themselves. Once, Mindy, a high powered New York lawyer, came up to us about a year after we had met her for the first time.

"Shya, Ariel, I have to tell you something really funny," she said. "You know how you always tell us that the voice we listen to in our heads is not us? Well, I just realized that when I first came to an evening and you said something to that effect, I sat in the back row thinking, *What voice? I don't understand what you are talking about. I don't have a voice. I don't hear anything.* I just realized that this was what you were talking about. The whole conversation I had privately, mentally, is the voice you were referring to. It took me a while before it dawned on me that this commentary wasn't me at all but just a conversation I was listening to."

"Ahh," Shya said to her, "Good for you. Now you have caught

it. Life is like a movie and your internal commentary is the soundtrack that is laid alongside the film. It is not a part of the film but something that is added."

"OK, Mindy," I said with a grin, "I have a riddle for you. If you aren't the voice in your head, who are you?"

Mindy's eyes scanned the ceiling as she computed the question. Her lips moved slightly as they reformed a ghost of the words, "If you aren't the voice in your head, who are you?"

"I don't know," she said slowly. "I guess you could say that if I am not the voice that is speaking, then I must be the one who listens. I am the person or being, the one who listens to the commentary."

I remember we all smiled as she hit on the truth. We just stood there enjoying each other's company for a moment as inside, our collective voices became fairly still.

The stillness that Monday evening, however, was anything but quiet. It was more like a river, which was swelling, and while the surface might have looked smooth, there was a raging current beneath.

When I was little, one of the books my mother read to me at naptime was "The Little Engine That Could". It is the story about a train that is trying to build enough steam to take a heavy load over a hill. He starts chugging along and he says, "I think I can, I think I can," and eventually he says, "I know I can, I know I can," and the Little Engine finally makes it.

As the fidgeting increased, I knew someone's desire to talk was about to outweigh their internal tapes. I could swear I heard that Little Engine getting closer. Maybe I could give things a boost.

"Well, we don't have to stay until 10. We could always end early if there is nothing left to talk about." I did my best to deliver this pronouncement with a straight face but I wasn't entirely successful.

"No, no, no! I have something to talk about. I guess I better start talking."

As Linda, a tall, lean woman in her late thirties began to speak I could tell that she was all stirred up. Of course, it is not difficult to tell with her. Linda was born in Germany and although she has been living in America for most of her adult life, her heritage can still be heard in her accent. When she is agitated or otherwise provoked, the accent becomes more pronounced.

"Shya, Ariel, I have to talk about something that is really bothering me."

And I guessed whatever 'it' was, was really bothering her, too, because as she said this, her face became chalky white. This is one of Linda's not-so-subtle visual clues that something is on her mind. But that night, although her face was pale, there was a fire in her eyes.

"I'm dating Dan and I am really enjoying it. I have never felt so good in my life."

"And this is really bothering you?" Shya asked with mock seriousness.

"No!" she said with a breathless grin as she looked at Dan. Their budding romance is one that gave me great pleasure, because these are two really great folks who had thought there was something wrong with themselves. They had never really been in love before, at least not the way they were with each other in that moment. Before meeting us, they had fairly well resigned themselves to the fact that finding a relationship would never happen.

"A couple of weeks ago you gave me a challenge, Ariel."

"I did?"

"Well, actually you both did. You asked, 'How good are you willing to have it be?' And you know what? It's been driving me crazy. I have started to see all of the little ways I sabotage myself. You know, like arriving just a few minutes late for a meeting I promised to be on time for just so I will be a little stressed for the whole thing. Or like with Dan."

"What about 'with Dan'?" Shya gently teased using the same inflection as Linda, which deflated the seriousness and brought a grin back to her face.

I guess now would be a good time to describe Linda's grin. It is wide and infectious. If all of us had faces that would register our thoughts and feelings as well as Linda's, the world would be a lot easier place to live in because there would be so few secrets.

"You know," Linda continued, "it just doesn't make sense to me. I mean, Dan loves me. He really loves me and this goes against every story I have ever told myself about who I am. Sometimes I find myself just wanting to get away from the intensity. I will find myself being sharp with him and although I see my meanness as I am doing it, I can't seem to help myself."

As Linda continued on about how her insensitivity got in the way of intimacy, Dan continued to gaze at her with warmth and humor and it looked to me as if he was proud to be in her company.

"Now wait a minute, Linda."

She stopped mid-sentence and looked at me blinking, "Yes?"

"Have you ever heard us tell you to give yourself a break?"

"Yes, I have but I am afraid that if I am not careful, I am going to blow it in this relationship."

"Have you asked Dan how it has been hanging out with you?" Shya asked.

"No." A little nervously Linda turned her gaze to meet Dan's and there could be no denying the love between them. Her shoulders began to relax.

Dan tilted his head and spoke in a clear voice, "Don't worry, Linda. I am not going anyplace. If I do, it is only because I am following you."

Most of the folks in the room began to melt into themselves along with Linda and Dan but I noticed another couple on the left who got tense and rigid.

Hmm, I thought, *something is brewing over there.*

As Linda and Dan held hands Shya and I did our best to short circuit some of the potential trauma in their relationship-building process.

"Linda," Shya began, "I have a few questions for you. Is this the best relationship you have had so far?"

This was an easy question. The answer flashed across her face with her smile. "Yes, absolutely!"

"Good. How about on the communication level, how is it doing there?"

"Well, you know, I find it is easier to speak with Dan than any person I have ever known."

The couple on the left looked even more tense. *Ahh, something they haven't been communicating.*

"You are lucky," Shya continued, "At least you are becoming aware of your mechanical behaviors early in the relationship. Most people don't realize what they are doing until they have built up hard feelings with their partner that they have to work through."

By now I knew that Shya had also noticed the couple on the left and was speaking to them along with Linda and Dan. It seemed to be working, too, because he was obviously striking a chord with them. I love groups for just that reason. Sometimes, it is so much easier for a person to sort out a problem when he or she is not on the spot. Linda's willingness to reveal herself was, unbeknownst to her, having a strong effect on others.

"At one point you took yourself away, Linda," Shya continued, "and didn't even know you were doing it. You thought that this was just part of your personality or the way you were. Now you are catching yourself becoming contracted as it is happening. If you don't beat on yourself when you see yourself retreating, then you open. Then, the next time you get snappish, you might catch it before you say something hurtful or before you take yourself away."

"Linda, Dan is not your victim," I said, "I'll bet, if you talk about it, you will discover that he is pulling back about the same time as you are. He might even be doing something geared to drive you away so he, too, can have some relief from the intensity of relating."

"That's true," Dan admitted. "Actually I haven't really noticed you taking yourself away but, in my last relationship, I did many things that bugged my partner."

Linda's face lit up as a thought occurred to her. "Yeah, actually there is something you do that makes me a little edgy. I hate it when you mother me. I mean, sometimes I feel like you want to take care of me and I don't feel like being taken care of."

By the end of the last sentence, she was looking intense, her features now stormy and Dan started to look worried like he might be in trouble.

"OK, so you both have a part to play in the dynamics of your relationship," Shya interjected which broke the spell and lightened the mood again.

"One of the most challenging things to realize in a relationship is that it is not a 50/50 deal. The health of the relationship is 100% Linda's responsibility from her point of view and 100% Dan's responsibility from his point of view."

"You know, I hate that!" Linda said with another of her disarming grins. "If I am having problems with Dan, I certainly want to have it be his fault, if not totally, at least mostly. I have heard you say this in other workshops and I know it is true when I apply it to my life, but I can't stand being wrong."

"I have some good news and some bad news for you, Linda," I replied, "It takes two to fight and only one to stop the fight."

The couple on the left were so uncomfortable by now that,

unbeknownst to them, they were practically jumping around in their seats. It reminded me a little of the Mexican jumping beans I kept in my desk drawer when I was eight or nine. When I held the small plastic box that contained them, the heat from my hand would make the worm inside get active and they would begin to jump. I guess the idea of 100% responsibility could make your temperature go up a notch when you have been collecting some really good evidence that your partner is the bad one in your relationship.

I decided I would flesh out the concept of responsibility and maybe this would make things easier for them.

"I mean it would be so easy, for example, for Linda to blame Dan or vice versa when things go awry, but that won't do either of them any good. Linda has always had the propensity to take herself away or get snappish and Dan has pushed to make others snap. She could get him to fix his behavior but sooner or later she'll be grouchy with someone else if she doesn't dissolve in herself the part that wants to lash out or take itself away. If she dissolves the urge to fight, then even if Dan pushes, she won't have to react. Instead, when something doesn't sit right with her, she will be self-empowered to communicate appropriately."

The couple on the left didn't like this news. They were thinking something like, *Easy for you to say but I ain't buying it.*

It's funny how sometimes people are fighting and they actually think they want to resolve the battle but, when faced with a solution, they will both argue to keep the fight going.

"Of course, Linda," Shya said, "what will make any problem between you and Dan nearly impossible to resolve is your agenda, your 6%. If you are determined to convince yourself and others that Dan is the culprit and that you have no part to play in the equation, if you are more interested in being right, the fight will never end. Not only that, fighting as a way of relating, may now be a part of your lifestyle, which you are afraid to lose. This lifestyle includes complaining that you don't want it to be this way. But then again, if it ended, you would have to think up whole new topics to discuss with your girlfriends."

"Yeah, that's true. I do have a tendency to gossip sometimes, especially when I am upset," Linda said. "I can see what you are saying about my tendency to be righteous and fight. But, if it means that this behavior will turn my relationship sour, I don't want to be right. I would rather be with Dan!"

As we continued on with the next question, I knew the fight was over between them, at least for the moment, and I hoped that now they had more tools to combat the war should it crop up again. The couple on the left was sure we were over-simplifying things but sometimes people have been known to see the validity of one of our foreign concepts later on. I rather doubted it with these two, but you never know.

There is one thing I am certain of, though, if a person wants to stop fighting, anything can be used as an excuse to finish the battle. But, if that same person wants to be right, if they are protecting their 6%, nothing, no matter how inspired, will be enough to have the conflict resolve. It was clear that this couple had so much invested in being right, that to give up making the other out to be the bad guy seemed like an unthinkable sacrifice. They were each listening to an old familiar tape loop. It was the one that ran the list of transgressions the other had done and the soundtrack went something like, *No, you don't understand, it really is his fault. You don't know him like I do. There was the time he...*

I know how challenging it can be to let go of the story that one's partner, boss, or parent is the source of misery in life. But I also know from experience, it is worth it.

WHY DO I WORRY ABOUT SILLY, SILLY THINGS?!

OVER THE YEARS, THE TWO OF US HAVE NOTICED THAT HOW AN individual thinks is normal to that person. So, if a person is depressed or worried, that is the way it is. But we have also realized that when a person lives in the moment and stops worrying, that becomes normal, too.

Recently our friend, Amy, came across an old diary of hers and was surprised to read about how her life used to be. Since she has discovered how to be present, regardless of the circumstances, she had forgotten that things were once so painful.

When we first met Amy (and eventually her husband, Andy) it

was at the prompting of our C.P.A. friend, Roger. He called us and said, "I just did something that I am not sure you are going to thank me for. I invited a woman to one of your evening groups because I thought she could really use it. She and her husband came to me for their taxes and I have never met two people who fight so much. They sat in my office and argued for the entire hour!"

Little did any of us know that Amy and Andy would meet us and use our approach to discover their brilliance. Nor could we have predicted that they would eventually become two of our closest friends.

Amy loaned us that diary so we could see her progression from pain to well-being. While there were glimpses of the person Amy has become, her magnificence was covered by a blanket of despair and worry. Amy has graciously written the following in which she shares excerpts of her journal. It demonstrates how transformation is both instantaneous and progressive. It is obvious that this intelligent woman couldn't 'understand' what was happening but she still had the courage to keep going. Amy gives us all a message of hope and encouragement.

142

My accountant said, "Cancel it! Just cancel it and come meet these two people." I was on the phone with my new C.P.A., complaining about my life and telling him I had made an appointment for that evening with a new therapist. I was feeling very depressed, a sense of desperation, worrying most of the time and basically, I could not go on living my life the way I was feeling.

So, in February of 1991, I listened to him, cancelled my appointment and went to meet the two people he suggested, Ariel and Shya Kane. Good Move! Now I don't worry much at all. I'm not depressed; I feel satisfied with everything and life is just pretty excellent.

Recently, while looking through some boxes, I found my old diary from those days. I had kept many journals and this one was number 24. As I leafed through the pages, I was shocked at how different my life is today from how it was when I wrote all of those diaries. It was fun and illuminating to remember how I had looked at my world and to see how my life transformed as I embraced the moment and risked going into the unknown. The difference between the entries that I made before I met Ariel and

Shya and after I met them amazes me.

When I opened my diary, I noticed a page that said in great big letters:

Why Do I Worry About Silly, Silly Things?!

It was the fall of 1990, I was 26 and I had all the things I wanted: I had a great job making excellent money on Wall Street at Shearson Lehman, a wonderful husband that I had recently married, and was in the process of getting my Masters Degree in Computer Science at NYU. I also owned a townhouse, worked out, so I was physically fit and I sang and played keyboards in a band.

Everything was in place – except me. I felt lonely, sad, old and worried. I thought all of the things that I had and all of the things I had achieved were supposed to make me satisfied. But the more I achieved and the more I had, the more feeling good eluded me. Here are excerpts of what I wrote:

> "September 28, 1990: Ok, here I am, I'm at a great job. Finally! I love it here at Shearson Lehman. I know I know – well it's about time!"

And, just a few days later...

> "October 1, 1990: Sometimes I get incredibly lonely. Is
> lonely the right word? I feel alone in this world. But
> I am not really alone, I have friends, I have family."

The New Year of 1991 came around and I started writing New Year's resolutions, trying to change what I felt was wrong. I was depressed and I kept trying to figure out why. At first I blamed it on the weather. Then, it was the new war we were in with Saddam Hussein. The winter, the war, I was trying to pin it on something.

That's when my accountant told me to cancel the appointment. In early February, I went to an evening seminar on "Being in the Moment" given by Ariel and Shya and I really liked it. I didn't understand it, but there was something there.

> "February 28, 1991: I have trouble being 'in the
> moment'. I don't want to be in the moment and lose
> me. I'm scared of what me really is. And then, even if
> I find me and go through a lot of pain to find me, what's
> the point? What's the point to life and does finding me
> have to be painful?"

I was afraid to really look at myself because I assumed that it would be painful. I didn't yet realize that the more I saw about myself, the easier life would become.

Then my birthday came. I was turning 27 and I felt depressed and old so I wrote a list of all the things that were bothering me.

"March 5, 1991 — My birthday:

1. I don't know how to let go and I mean really let go, not just say I am letting go.

2. I worry too much.

3. I feel guilty too much.

4. I always expect a lot out of friends and then I blame them and/or myself when they don't meet my expectations.

5. I get scared and I have made some wrong choices.

6. I'm scared to be alone so I make a lot of friends. Their friendship is important to me because I don't want to be alone.

7. I take everything too personally.

8. I'm scared to die. Everything is temporary and this fact hurts me. It hurts me a lot.

I'm 27 almost 30 – and I feel almost empty, scared, torn and hateful."

At this point, I had attended only one evening seminar with the Kanes, but I wanted more personal attention so I decided to have a private session with them on March 20th.

Here's the entry I wrote the day after:

"First day of Spring, yes!

Last night I went to see Shya and Ariel. I was tense. I was nervous. It was wonderful & emotional. I cried and I laughed. I don't understand exactly what happened but do I have to?"

And then on May 2, 1991:

"WOW WOW WOW

That's how I feel – WOW!

I don't know, it's so strange – really strange. Things are changing in me rotating, moving. I'm beginning to feel like I want to live again – I'm beginning to feel I want to be alive – alive!

Over the past two months something has changed in me – I don't know what. I've gone to three of their New York City evening seminars, one weekend workshop, and two private sessions and it's been amazing – scary. But now I don't feel scared.

Yesterday I did. I'm different today – every day, every moment."

And on May 23, 1991:

"I feel my world has rotated a little and I'm looking out another window – there is so much to see."

This was an exciting time. I have to admit that I didn't understand how it was that my life was improving. Eventually, I stopped trying to figure out why. I just let myself enjoy the process and be grateful for the results. Then over Memorial Day weekend, my husband and I decided to do our first workshop together with the Kanes...and on June 20th I wrote:

"So much has happened! Workshop w/ Shya & Ariel in Phoenicia – EXCELLENT!!"

After this workshop, both my husband and I felt more in love and more in sync than ever. We started to do more workshops together and go to the evening seminars together. We were learning about each other and ourselves and life was getting easier.

Here's an entry from August 5, 1991 after my husband and I had done a *Freedom to Breathe* course with the Kanes:

> "A few days after the breath group, I had a lot of thoughts in my head. Then work got really busy and the thoughts drifted away.
>
> I'm learning to live in the present. A few years ago, if someone told me it is beneficial to live in the present, I would have laughed at them or even scowled at them. It was against everything I believed in.
>
> I worry less – I hear my mind – I'm learning it's not me – they are just thoughts.
>
> I hear crickets and the waves a little – the air conditioning blowing thru the vent. This is life."

And basically, the last entry of my diary went like this:

> "I've been watching the eagles soar in my heart.

I've been feeling the waves of passion. Do you feel what I feel? Do you see the love in my heart?"

Since that time, my life has continually gotten more rich and wonderful. My husband, Andy, and I are closer than ever and we've been married for more than a decade. We now have a beautiful son and our own Web/Internet company, TAG Online. We work together side-by-side, day in and day out and we love it. Andy and I continue to work with the Kanes by doing their courses, having them as personal coaches, and consultants to our business. We discover more about each other and ourselves and life is very exciting.

I haven't written in a diary since. I don't feel the urge to. Why do I worry about silly, silly things? I don't anymore.

THE GENDER WAR

PEOPLE TALK ABOUT THE GENDER WAR BUT THEY DON'T SEE THE subtle and not so subtle ramifications of unaware behaviors that have been handed down to us through the eons of time. There used to be a strong and clear division of labor between men and women. The men worked together and the women worked together which then created two separate subcultures within the culture as a whole.

This societal division was not equitable. It was fostered in a time when humanity was openly savage and brutal, where 'might' meant 'right' and where the larger of the species dominated those under their rule. In most cultures, men, who were stronger and more powerful, ran the show. There was only cooperation regarding survival and the needs of survival. The men hung out with the men and the women hung out with the women.

And that   1s of years. Humanity has
only rece   y of creating environments
that a   'n the last 100 years the
tri⅃   ur cultural heritage
have ⅃   ⅃nology and a shifting
of social values.   go, one could not survive outside
the tribal or fami.   But, with the advent of modern
technologies, humanity has been thrown irrevocably into a new
time where gender does not determine your social station for the
rest of your life.

There was a time in this society when a woman could only be a teacher, a librarian, a nurse, a secretary, a clerk, a housewife or a mother. The possibility for a woman to become a doctor, a lawyer, a bank executive, a plumber or police officer was slim to none. Until just recently, these professions and many others were off limits to women. Now they are available, but there is social baggage of resentments and prejudices that have been handed down about what is 'woman's work' and what a woman is good for.

Traditionally, a woman's identity was tied to her role as part of a relationship in which she was expected to maintain and care for a family and men's roles were more associated with having a job and tied to their vocation.

If you want your relationship to flourish, it is important that you become aware of the stereotypes and prejudices that are ingrained in your thoughts that are the background over which your current relationship is played. There are many different facets to the war between the genders and we are going to outline them so that you can become aware of them as factors that can undermine an otherwise healthy relationship.

BEHAVIOR DESIGNED TO KEEP THE OTHER OFF BALANCE IN ORDER TO MAINTAIN DOMINANCE OR THE IDEA OF SUPERIORITY

A couple once came to us for counseling because they had read some of our articles and wanted help with their relationship. The four of us sat down and we asked what was happening between them. Steve and Terri, who had been married for almost 30 years, started to lay out the source of their strife. We were surprised at the particulars.

Terri spoke first. She leaned forward and earnestly said, "Well, our first Christmas together, I bought and wrapped for Steve 27 different presents and gave them to him. He didn't even give me one present that year. I couldn't believe it. How could he have been so thoughtless not to know how important Christmas is and not even to have bothered to get me one, single present? This has been the story of our relationship. He has been thoughtless from the beginning. Not only that, I make the money. He basically only walks the dog. You would think that after all these years he would be less selfish and pay some attention to me, but no. That's why we have come to you two. I am hoping you can help him see how to finally take care of me for a change."

Steve's side of the story was equally embattled and even more surprising than Terri's. When asked what he wanted out of our time together, he said he felt he should make something clear. Next to Steve was a canvas tote bag, which he had brought along to the session. He reached inside and pulled out a well-worn, framed photo of Terri in her wedding dress and said, "See how thin she used to be? Can you believe how fat she has gotten?"

Truthfully, we were shocked by the breadth and depth of their battle. We inquired whether Steve had brought the photo

especially to our meeting because it was something in particular
he wished to share with us and he said, "No, I carry this picture
around with me because I want people to know just what I have
to put up with."

Over the course of the hour we spent with them, we were able
to facilitate a spontaneous reconciliation, where they laid down
their weapons, at least for awhile. But, when the need to be right
is more important than the desire to have a great life and a loving
relationship, then the need to be right will win and the war will
ultimately continue.

We tell you about Steve and Terri because, even though the story
is true, they seem to be a larger than life rendition of how many
couples fight or relate. When you see an acute version of this
type of fight, it is easier to find the subtle ways in which you may
have unwittingly undermined relationships in a similar manner.

If you want to attack a woman, one effective tool is to criticize
her attractiveness, weight or appearance. An effective tool to
attack a man is to criticize his ability to produce or provide. If
you wish for harmony between each other, it is important to be
aware that there are culturally ingrained hot spots with your

partner. If you know what they are you don't have to unwittingly or purposefully trigger them.

FAMILY TRADITIONS

You are probably familiar with the term, 'war between the sexes' but have you thought to investigate all of the fronts on which the gender war appears and is fought? It is essential to bring awareness to all of the ways you have unknowingly been recruited into the fight if you want a magical relationship.

The two of us were once on our boat, slowly cruising through a marina on the way to the gas dock. From a distance we heard angry voices shouting at one another. The man's voice said something like, "You never..." and the woman's voice was yelling, "You always..." at the same time. As we motored past their boat, which was tied to the dock, we saw that the woman was seated busily filing her nails while shouting sarcastically over her shoulder at her mate and he was standing glowering behind her, beer in hand, yelling down at her back. The name of the boat was (and we are not making this up) "Family Tradition".

You have learned a lot of your attitudes toward the opposite sex, including body postures, tone of voice and other ways of relating, from your family. If you want to see how you engage in the gender war, simply dispassionately look at your own family life. If you can look at anything from your own childhood, without judging what you see, you can begin to unwire the legacy that is passed down from generation to generation.

Don't forget the first of the Three Principles of Transformation that we discussed in earlier chapters: What you resist persists and grows stronger. If you are judging the way your parents related and you have vowed to do it differently, then you will produce one of two ways of relating. As you get older you either will become more and more like the parent whom you resisted or when faced with conflict, for instance, you will do the opposite. If he or she was a person who yelled, and you promised yourself you would never yell at your spouse, then in times of stress you will find you may suddenly 'snap' and yell at your partner or you will become quiet and withdraw. Neither position creates the balance people are craving.

CASUAL CONVERSATION
AND GOSSIP CAN BE CORROSIVE

People who are fighting with the opposite sex will often try to
gather agreement for their point of view. This is such an
automatic behavior that the prejudicial viewpoint will slip
naturally into conversation unnoticed. If you don't bring
awareness to this condition, it will erode even the best relationship.

Here is an example as told from Shya's personal experience:
Recently I went into a store to buy a piece of electronics
equipment. As the fellow behind the counter was filling out the
paperwork, he mentioned he was having a bad day. I said, "I'm
sorry to hear that."

"Yeah," the salesman, Bart, continued, "I made the mistake of
taking my wife's car keys with me to work and now she is
bitching at me that she has to walk everywhere."

I didn't say much to his comment and the transaction continued.
As I handed him my credit card he noticed that the magnetic
strip on the back of the card was worn.

"Oh," Bart said, "This looks just like my wife's card, it's all worn out because she uses it so much. Actually, she had her wallet stolen in New York last month but I haven't reported it because the thief is spending less than she was."

Nonplused, I looked at Bart. I think he expected me to have a hearty laugh at his wife's expense because he said, "That was a joke, Mr. Kane. That was supposed to be a joke." I told Bart that I didn't find it funny and that this type of divisive commentary was probably one of the reasons why he and his wife were fighting.

Here is another example of how war between the sexes can happen as told from Ariel's personal experience:

When Shya and I moved to our current home, we went to a new dental office. While Shya was having his teeth examined by the dentist, the dental hygienist, Carrie, came into the room and said to him, "Your better half is finished and waiting for you." Shya said, "No, that's not right. She isn't my better half, she is my partner and my friend."

I didn't hear this interaction because I was in another examination room. However, after Shya responded to her, the hygienist came back to the room where I was seated, leaned over conspiratorially and said, "I just told your husband that his better half was waiting for him."

I sat there for an instant, feeling uneasy debating what to do next. I just couldn't let the remark pass. Not because I wanted to change Carrie's point of view but because I felt that if I kept quiet it would be the same as telling her I agreed with her perspective. Unwilling to be a co-conspirator against men, I replied, "Excuse me, what you just said is inaccurate. I am not his better half, I am his partner." She got very quiet. When our dentist came into my room with Shya, I greeted them both and said, "Oh, by the way, Carrie just told me what she said to you and I told her I wasn't your better half but your partner." Stunned, the doctor said, "That's amazing, your husband just said the exact same thing."

Carrie had come into my room to enroll me in her point of view that women were better than men. If I am the better half, what does that make him? Certainly not my equal. Even though I don't share her point of view, if I hadn't said anything, I might have gone home looking to see in what ways he was inferior or less. I am fairly certain that Carrie is unaware of how she maligns men. It was just casual conversation on her part. However, even casual conversation, if unexamined, can take its toll on an otherwise healthy relationship.

In these last accounts, Ariel chose to say something to Carrie and Shya also said something to Bart. You don't always need to speak up, but sometimes you do. Either way, you'll know what is appropriate by how you feel. The important aspect is to notice and become aware that other people's opinions affect your relationship.

Next is an example, as told by Ariel, about another way casual conversations in a public environment impacted our relationship: A few years ago, I went to a nearby series of one-hour step classes, a form of aerobic exercise. I went to these classes three or four times a week and there was a group of women that regularly attended. A kind of camaraderie developed and the ladies idly chatted before, during and after the class. I soon discovered that if I did not pay attention, I not only exercised my body but also the socially ingrained prejudice against men.

Here are a few snippets of the usual conversations:

"Wow, Stacey, you look really good. You're really losing weight!"

"Yeah, you may notice but my husband doesn't. He never notices anything. You know how men are…"

"I'm going on vacation in a couple of weeks to Mexico and I want to get in really good shape so I can look sexy and gorgeous. I can't wait, it's going to be great. It's just Julie and me. No husbands, no kids!"

"My husband, Steve, and I had a fight this morning. His real name is Hemorrhoid." (The instructor made this comment while teaching the class!)

After class I would come home and if there had been men-bashing comments, something would invariably change in my demeanor towards Shya. Eventually, it became a game that Shya and I played where he would say, "How did they get you this morning?" and I would identify and relate all of the seemingly innocent negative comments that had been made about men. It became a follow up exercise to my aerobic exercise. By simply identifying the daily war, I didn't have to become a part of it. By attending classes I was strengthening my muscles, coordination and building endurance. After class, I strengthened the muscle of being able to stay true to my reality and values in relationship to Shya in particular and men in general.

STEREOTYPES, UNEXAMINED,
CONTRIBUTE TO THE WAR

Women often suppose that men are prejudiced against women and men suppose that women are prejudiced against men, but generally neither gender looks to see the prejudices they have about themselves. If you don't become aware of your own internal prejudices about people of your own sex, you will unwittingly assign these prejudices to your partner. In other words, you will blame your partner for your own unexamined viewpoint.

In order to see and neutralize the gender war in all its forms, you need to become aware of the attitudes and stereotypes you have unwittingly gathered about the opposite sex, as well as the attitudes and stereotypes you have collected about your own gender.

In this day and age, both men and women can perform most any job. However, in each person's background, they have been exposed to cultural norms and eventually these generalities become superimposed over reality.

Here is an example of what to look for:

In the anecdote about the dental assistant, Carrie, do you recall that the dentist was surprised that we each, independently, said that we were partners? Did you have a mental picture of this interaction?

Our dentist is a woman. Most people, when told this story, visualize a man. Again, this is not in and of itself a problem. As we said previously, the mind pulls comparisons from what it already knows and has experienced. It conjures images from our past and that past itself can prejudice what is possible in the future.

If we were to talk about children being raised by one parent while the other traveled as a high-powered executive, chances are the automatic image would be that of a woman at home and a man in the workplace, even if the story were really about a stay-at-home dad and a working mom.

PREJUDICES, UNEXAMINED, CONTRIBUTE TO THE WAR

A client of ours, Peter, thought he was a fair-minded individual who had nothing against women. He had been critical of his father for looking down on his mother and treating her as less. As a medical doctor, Peter felt he had, by virtue of education and experience, gotten 'beyond that'. He even went so far as to volunteer, "I don't think of women as second class citizens." Yet, when we spoke with Peter, his strong biases against females kept being revealed.

When Peter talked to us about his time in the military, he commented that he honestly felt having women in combat situations was dangerous. He explained that having women in combat was not the optimum solution because their upper body strength is not enough to carry a fallen comrade out of harm's way. This idea may sound reasonable but, when Peter spoke about this potential situation he said, "I can't believe they would let such weaklings into a combat zone."

Here is another example that illuminated Peter's unexamined point of view about women:

As he began to investigate how he viewed females, Peter told us about a comment he made, apparently in jest, to his 13 year old daughter, Vivian. One day at a local shopping mall they passed another man and his four girls. Peter told us he said, "Vivian, look at how sad that man is. He only has daughters and would give anything if one of them were a son." While Vivian tried to laugh at the 'joke' Peter noticed that she was offended and things were less easy between them after that. This and other comments of this nature had caused a rift between them.

Most people are prejudiced against the idea of being prejudiced. In Peter's case, he thought it was better to think of females as equals and so he was hiding from himself all of the ways he held them in disdain. His prejudicial point of view was so normal to him that it became transparent, like water to a fish.

We told Peter an old anecdote, which allowed him to get a glimpse of his prejudices on his own. Here is that story and the ensuing conversation:

A young boy was playing ball in the yard and when it rolled into the street, he darted out between two cars to retrieve it. A car, coming down the street, didn't see the boy and struck him. The boy's father had seen the accident from the living room window but it had happened so quickly, he was powerless to stop it. Rushing outside, he scooped his son into his arms and bade the motorist to quickly drive them to the hospital that was, mercifully, only a few blocks away. When they pulled up to the emergency entrance, the man ran inside with his son in his arms. In the emergency room, it was determined that the boy needed surgery because he had sustained internal injuries. But the surgeon, upon seeing the child said, "I can't operate on this boy, he is my son!"

"How is this possible?" we asked Peter. Our medical friend had a bright and facile mind so we encouraged him to look and see what was obvious to us about this story. He began to explore the possibilities.

"The father who carried his boy into the emergency room actually was employed as a surgeon at the hospital. He just happened to be home to see the accident rather than at work," was the first answer that came to Peter's mind.

"Not the true end to this story or the answer to this riddle," we said. "The man was standing with his son when the surgeon said 'I can't operate on this boy, he is my son!' Keep looking," we encouraged Peter.

"The surgeon was the real father of the boy and the man who was in the living room was just the stepfather."

"Good try, but that is not correct either. Keep looking," we said. Then we again reiterated the last sentence of the story where the surgeon said, "I can't operate on this boy, he is my son!" Again we asked Peter, "How is this possible?"

"OK, the surgeon was the boy's father, more in the spiritual sense and for some religious reason felt he couldn't interfere with God's plan."

"No, that's not the answer," we replied.

"Well, the man just thought he was the boy's father."

Eventually we told Peter the end of the story because, given his perspective, the true ending was not a possibility. The answer to this perplexing question of "How is it possible?" is this:
The surgeon could not operate on the boy, because *she* was the boy's mother.

Peter was truly shocked. As a physician, he was working in a hospital where there were both male and female doctors. His unexamined prejudices had clouded his vision.

Again, as we mentioned before, prejudice itself is not a bad thing if you are aware of it. If you know you have a bias, you can be responsible to include it and not act through it as if it were true.

We encouraged Peter to keep noticing his prejudices. We asked him to notice when he thought of women in a demeaning, sarcastic or dismissive manner, without being hard on himself when he saw things about his behavior that he believed to be negative. We further encouraged him to forgive himself for the unkind, unaware things he had said and done in the past because he could not go back and undo them.

A few weeks later, Peter's uncle died and he attended a family gathering and funeral. When he returned, Peter told us of the unexamined point of view about women that he discovered in his familial culture. Peter's uncle had married a woman in 1933 but they were unable to have children. Actually, how it was looked at in the family was that 'she' was unable to have children. So, the uncle got a divorce and married another lady. However, the uncle continued to have sexual intimacy with both. Soon, both women got pregnant and "as luck would have it, they both had girls, but neither could give him a son".

Prior to Peter investigating his culturally ingrained attitudes towards women, this statement would have been casual conversation that was simply part of the fabric of his life. However, with his newfound awareness, Peter began to see what had been hidden from him. The seeing of it allowed him to operate in a manner that was honest to his own personal feelings and values.

Within a couple of days after Peter returned from the funeral, he came into the kitchen one morning and saw Vivian enjoying her breakfast cereal. In that moment, he saw what a lovely woman she was becoming and was so proud of her. Here is what he thought to say: *Gee, Vivian, in another culture, you would be valuable enough that I could get at least 10 camels for you.*

Peter was startled that his first inclination was to say something that demeaned his daughter rather than simply letting Vivian know how pretty she looked. With awareness, he didn't need to mechanically blurt out something that would certainly cause more friction between them.

As Peter became aware of his prejudices, without judging what he saw, transformations began to take place. Out of the blue, his daughter, with whom he had had a strained relationship for several years, spontaneously came to hang out with him and watch a movie in the den. Soon they started to have very real conversations again, as opposed to behaving like two strangers living in the same house.

The unexamined gender war affects not only the relationship you have between you and yourself or you and your mate, it affects how you relate to everyone in your life. By simply observing your automatic attitudes without judging what you see, your way of relating will transform in a profound manner.

CULTURAL BIASES, UNEXAMINED, CONTRIBUTE TO THE WAR

Peter discovered that his attitudes about women were something that was not only a part of his family's views, but also something that was ingrained in the culture in which he was raised. It hadn't occurred to him to investigate the perspective of his culture. Like most people, he didn't stop to see that his reality had been defined by the unexamined attitudes around him as he grew up. Initially he had blamed his parents for their prejudices, not stopping to realize that they had been dipped into a cultural dye that had colored their worldview.

One of our clients, Lisa, began to become aware of her ingrained cultural biases when she came to one of our business communication courses. The assignment was to give a two-minute talk on something that was inspirational. The topic didn't matter. This was an exercise in self-expression designed to allow the speaker to inspire the listeners with his or her enthusiasm.

When Lisa's turn came, she chose a subject that was truly heartfelt. She spoke about her two year old daughter, Tanya. She let the listeners know that while she enjoyed managing a department of 30 professionals, coming home to her child was the best part of her day. Lisa really enjoyed the evening ritual of feeding, bathing and playing with Tanya before it was time for her to sleep. Watching Tanya learn and grow and take her first steps were some of the most meaningful moments of Lisa's life.

This is certainly true for many mothers who are in the workforce. However, the more Lisa spoke, the more her audience became aware that there was a glaring omission in Lisa's account of her time with her child.

Here is a piece of Lisa's presentation. Perhaps you can see it for yourself:

"About three years ago, I decided I wanted a child, so I went out and got one. Her name is Tanya and she is now two years old and I love her more than anything. I was afraid to have children but I am very happy that I got one because she is the light of my life. The best part of the day is when I come home from work and she is there. I love to play with her and give her my full attention. She really loves to eat cheerios and is going through a stage where eating cottage cheese is like being in heaven. Bath time is one of my favorite times, too. She squeals and splashes and smells so good. She is so very alive."

Lisa went on to talk about more of her activities with Tanya but people in the course grew more and more confused. Sitting across the room during this presentation, was another course participant, Lisa's husband, John. Soon the other participants began to wonder if the couple had adopted the baby. Another theory one person had while listening to Lisa talk was that she had already had the child before she met John and that they were only recently married.

At the end of the talk, Lisa was gently given feedback and asked a few questions. She was truly astonished that her story made it sound as if she were a single parent and that John was not the biological father of their child. She soon realized that she didn't even mention her partner was at home participating in the day-to-day events that she described. The fact that Lisa had totally eradicated John from her inspirational talk about caring for Tanya gave her food for thought.

The next day, Lisa and John had a private coaching session with us. We were not surprised to find that there were challenges in their marriage, but what did surprise us was how actively Lisa was looking to see her part in the dynamics of their relationship.

As she looked at her life and the culture she came from, Lisa realized that there was a strong dismissal of men by all of the females in the community. She had come from a culture that was matriarchal and men were held as the lesser. Over the course of the session with us, she spontaneously identified ways that she dismissed John or treated him as inconsequential either in her words or by her actions. Both Lisa and John became excited by what she saw.

A few days later, we got an email from her. When Lisa returned to work, she saw that the mechanical behavior of dismissing men had been in full force with her male staff members. She immediately noticed that she had been listening more attentively and relating better with the women on her staff.

Before Lisa was aware of her own unexamined cultural bias, she had unwittingly segregated her current work community into a hierarchy of worth-more and worth-less. This simple awareness translated into immediate, positive results. By bringing her attention to including men and listening to what they had to say, Lisa quickly saw staff morale, teamwork and productivity increase.

This newfound awareness also had a dramatic impact on her love relationship. John saw that when Lisa was dismissive, it didn't mean that she was angry. He realized that this was just a part of her cultural heritage. When he didn't take her actions so personally, tensions eased. Immediately, their daughter was more open and playful with John. At age two, Tanya was already looking to Lisa as a role model for how to behave with men. As Lisa included John, it became easier for Tanya to include him as well.

The transformational effects of Lisa simply seeing how she was relating to her environment, without judging herself for what she saw, were truly profound and instantaneous.

E X E R C I S E S

THE GENDER WAR

1. As you watch television, pay particular attention to the commercials. Notice how the producers use and perpetuate the gender war to sell their products.

2. When you are in a checkout line, at work, the gym or other places where you would engage in or overhear casual conversation, notice if the dialogue contains sentiment that is either pro- or anti-male or female.

3. See if you can catch yourself when you erroneously make gender assumptions such as dentists are male and stay-at-home parents are female. Even if your own doctor is a female, look to see if when the subject of 'doctor' shows up in conversation, your mind still automatically inserts a male into the picture.

4. When you are in your community, such as work, places of worship, school and other places where people meet and share ideas, become aware of the cultural attitudes toward men, women and relationships.

RELATIONSHIP SPLITTERS

THERE IS A PHENOMENON THAT IS SO PREVALENT AND SO normal that it goes largely unnoticed, yet it remains one of the strongest impediments to creating and maintaining a healthy, loving relationship. Over the years, the two of us have seen many different variations of this mechanical behavior and rather organically, a term for what we have observed has emerged. We call it 'relationship splitters'. It is a behavior that is first seen between children and their parents and it expands into later life. It may be very innocent at first but, if left unexamined, it will destroy the possibility of having a magical relationship.

It is important when investigating this automatic way of relating that you are grounded in your anthropological outlook and non-judgmental way of seeing. If you misidentify relationship splitting as a 'bad' thing, you will not be able to see all the nuances of your own ways of relating and you will develop a lack of compassion for others who exhibit this behavior.

In this chapter are several anecdotes that illustrate different relationship splitting scenarios. There are so many variations of this phenomenon that it is virtually impossible to cover them all but we will present some of the archetypical themes so that you can learn to identify them in your own life.

RUPERT

There was a concert pianist, Rupert, who frequented our weekly evening groups in New York City. He made it a habit to sit in the back and he generally spoke up during the evening. It was very fascinating to watch the ripples of avid interest and extreme dislike that went through the room whenever he spoke. The women would sigh and dream of going to one of Rupert's concerts at Carnegie Hall, and the men would bristle and flash annoyed looks at one another. Then later, in private, disagreements would crop up between couples when they attempted to have even casual conversations about Rupert. One of the hallmarks of these interactions was the fact that the woman in the couple would not want to hear her husband or boyfriend's perspective and she felt compelled to defend Rupert.

With a little coaching these couples came to see that it was impossible for each to experience what the other was experiencing. It was as if Rupert was sending signals on two different wavelengths. The men discovered that they shouldn't feel frustrated that the women didn't 'see through' Rupert's presentation to see how competitive and divisive he was. The women learned to question the situation when they felt compelled to defend another man against their spouse or boyfriend. The act of needing to defend the 'poor, misunderstood' fellow against the 'bad man' became a signal to look for the mechanics of a relationship splitter in action.

Once a man came up to Ariel in one of our groups and said, "Are you doing your makeup differently? It looks really good tonight." Apparently this compliment was an innocuous statement but Ariel found herself thinking, *Shya doesn't notice me doing my makeup differently.* We spoke of this interaction privately and began to realize that this man regularly was attentive to the women in relationships while avoiding the single ladies. When a man is in competition with his father, he will attempt to be a 'better husband' to his mother or any woman who is in a relationship. And if a woman is in competition with her mother, she will try to be the 'better wife'. Often a woman who is a relationship splitter will send nonverbal signals, *Wouldn't you rather be with me? I am younger, prettier, sexier and more attentive than your wife.*

179

JACK, LESLIE & PHILLIP

Leslie and Jack were married for 14 years and had three kids. Work was stressful for Jack and things were rough at times. But they were normal folks trying to get by, raising their family to the best of their abilities. At some point in the marriage, Phillip, a foreign exchange student from Europe came to live with them for a school year. Prior to his arrival, Jack and Leslie had difficulties communicating and fought from time to time but they were doing their best to resolve it. After Phillip arrived, however, things dramatically changed. He became a confidant and friend to Leslie. He listened attentively when she spoke, and when Jack had to work long hours, Leslie and he would sit around the kitchen table and be 'best friends'. Of course, since Phillip was only a boy and not a romantic interest, Leslie didn't catch the signals that by confiding in Phillip, she was distancing herself from her relationship with Jack. Things that would normally be bottled up inside until they were addressed and completed with her husband now had an outlet elsewhere. This seemingly innocent relationship precipitated a seemingly sudden divorce. From Jack's point of view, Leslie was less available and he found himself being angry. He had no idea that Leslie and Phillip's relationship was precipitating many of his feelings of inadequacy and estrangement. All he knew was, he wanted a divorce.

Phillip had recreated in his new environment the relationship he had with his mother and father at home. For as long as Phillip could remember, he and his mother were best friends while, in his opinion, his father was cold, aloof and distant. As a rule, Phillip had a much easier time relating to women than men.

Phillip is a classic version of a relationship splitter. He finds himself attracted to or befriending people of the opposite sex who are already in a relationship. Just like in his earlier home life, he is committed to proving that he would be a better, more attentive and caring husband than the other person's actual spouse.

Let's look a little further at the dynamics between Leslie and Phillip. Sometime after her divorce, Leslie began dating again. After a couple of years Leslie finally found a fellow with whom she developed a serious relationship. Then, after not having heard from Phillip in several years, she suddenly received a call from him asking to come back and visit. She agreed, but when Phillip stayed in her house, Leslie and her beau had their first argument, and it was explosive. This disagreement led to a break up. After a year of being separate, Leslie and her boyfriend decided to give it another try. Within a day, Phillip called again and asked to stay at Leslie's house for part of his vacation.

There frequently seems to be a psychic connection between relationship splitters and the people to whom they are attracted. We are suggesting that the timing of Phillip's calls were not merely coincidental, but the result of an uncanny ability that many people have to be a consistent divisive influence in relationships.

JOAN

We found another classic example of a relationship splitter in Joan who came to one of our relationship seminars interested in finding someone with whom she could build a life, someone she could marry. During the course of the weekend Joan revealed that she traditionally had a history of dating married men and she was tired of this lifestyle. So we did an experiment. Since Joan didn't know many of the 70 or so people in the room, we thought it would be interesting to see whom she found attractive. We asked her to quickly, without much thought, look around the room and point out the men she found appealing. So she said, "I find you, you and you," etc. and she worked her way around the room, skipping those men whom she felt no pull towards. When she was done, we realized that every man Joan felt an interest in or drawn towards was a man already married or in a committed relationship. All of those that she skipped were single, available (and attractive) men.

Joan and her mother, historically, had had a tumultuous relationship with each other and Joan had never dated someone who was truly available. She found that she automatically gravitated to men who were already connected to another woman. Through our experiment and the resulting dialogue, Joan was able to see that at a very young age she had unwittingly committed herself toward being the 'better wife'. This unexamined competition with her mother was then eventually played out with all women and all relationships.

When unexamined, this way of relating becomes a lifestyle that follows the relationship splitter through all of his or her interactions and will continue unabated unless it is seen without judgment. In Joan's case, this was challenging because she did not like that she was attracted only to married men and yet she still found herself justifying why it was OK to date them. *I am just taking care of him because his wife is not good to him* and *He is just staying with her to not hurt the kids,* are just two of the stories she would tell herself. It hadn't occurred to Joan that her very presence had an impact on the way the man she was dating related to his wife and she to him.

THE RELATIONSHIP WITH YOURSELF:
JOEL AND BOB

There is one further type of relationship splitter that is probably the most challenging. This is the individual who divides you from being in relationship with yourself. When you are out of relationship with yourself, all of your interactions with others suffer as well.

Here is an example:

After many years of attempting to make what had devolved into a loveless marriage work, Joel and his wife Karen got a divorce. At the time of their breakup, Joel and Karen had a country home that they had bought and renovated, adding many amenities and personal touches. It had been a retreat for the couple and a place where they had enjoyed time with their son, Tim. They had also developed a community of friends over the summers they had spent there. So, during the divorce, one of the more challenging questions was deciding what to do with this property. It had many sentimental attachments for everyone involved. Initially Joel found himself longing for the sense of family, community and stability that this location had once offered. But, since his relationship with Karen was over, he put the country home behind him. He found new, unexplored country locales to spend time with his son so that they could still enjoy the outdoors together.

As Joel's life moved on, the country home fell into the background. He started a new relationship with a woman who adored him and his son and life was good as they moved forward as a new family unit.

Then one day Joel went for a meal with an old friend, Bob, who began asking him questions about his life.

"Do you miss the country home?" Bob asked.

Joel replied, "No not really. Tim and I have been going to other great places together. Just last month we spent two weeks in Vermont and it is really beautiful there."

"But don't you miss all of your old friends and the great screened-in porch you put on the front of your house? What about the convenience of leaving the city and an hour later being at your own place?"

Joel still let Bob know that the country home was history and that he had moved on.

However, Bob kept asking questions designed to reconnect Joel to the past and those questions painted a picture of 'the good old days'. Even though the times at the country home with his ex had been anything but good for the last number of years, the line of questioning kept directing Joel back into thinking he might have made a mistake with his life choices.

The next day, Joel felt generally irritable and when he saw his girlfriend he was distant and reserved. It wasn't until the couple spoke about the abrupt change in his attitude that they discovered that the conversation with Bob had started Joel down a path of self-recrimination and doubt. It had infused him with the idea that he might have made a mistake by getting out of the marriage with Karen. Upon looking further, Joel and his girlfriend realized that Bob was hanging onto a loveless, embattled marriage himself and was threatened that Joel had the courage to end a relationship that wasn't working. Bob was trying to encourage Joel to go back to his old life because it was more comfortable than looking at what wasn't working in his own marriage.

The two of us have found that people often give advice through a filter of their own fears. Well-meaning friends often caution others to not go too fast or too far. These friends tell themselves that they are only concerned for the happiness of the person they are advising but, in fact, they are really counseling others to not go for their dreams. If a person is afraid of looking at what isn't working in his or her own relationship and life, then the advice will be tainted in support of inactivity or holding on to the status quo.

STELLA

Here is another version of how your relationship with yourself can be eroded:

Stella has a passion for riding horses and her husband Steve is passionate about fly fishing. So they plan their vacations in places where they can do both. Last year they booked a week at a dude ranch with lots of trout streams. Even though Stella had her own horse, Dusty, at home, she felt it would be an excellent time to relax and learn new skills that she could bring home and teach him. Steve was looking forward to days of wandering down trout streams and having the luxury of spending the evenings with Stella. The plan was a good one but they didn't account for the influence the other guests and the proprietors of the dude ranch would have upon their relationship.

This ranch, owned and run by a couple, tended to attract mainly female guests. So, in the evening Stella and Steve would come to dinner and many of the women there would comment on how they would love it if their husbands would join them on vacation, but there really was an undercurrent of discomfort at having a man in their midst. It was as if Stella had invited the enemy on vacation. She found herself wanting to be liked by the other women and without realizing it, started rejecting Steve. But, not only did she reject Steve, she started rejecting her whole lifestyle as if she were doing her life wrong. She even began to be embarrassed that she worked in a big city rather than living in a rural area.

When Stella returned home from her trip, she found herself inordinately annoyed with people in general. She no longer wanted to chat with the local newspaper vendor or the fellow who sold her coffee in the morning. She began judging her job and coworkers. Nothing appeared right anymore. *Perhaps,* she thought, *I should just quit everything and move to the country.* And an odd thing happened. She was no longer passionate about riding her treasured friend, Dusty. She began to say things like, "I have to go ride the horse". The heart connection Stella had between herself and everyone and everything in her environment had been disrupted.

In an individual consulting session with us, Stella and Steve took on an anthropological point of view and non-judgmentally looked at what had happened to interfere so dramatically with their relationship and with Stella's relationship to herself and to her life in general. They saw that, while at the dude ranch, she had ignored the undercurrent of anti-men sentiment amongst the other guests because she wanted to be liked. They also saw that the husband and wife who ran the ranch bickered as a way of life and were competitive with each other. Stella had shut her eyes to the discomfort of being around them.

By simply seeing and recognizing that in her attempt to fit in she had inadvertently rejected her own truth, Stella was immediately reconnected to herself, her husband and even her horse. With simple recognition and without being hard on herself for getting lost in the first place, her sense of well-being came flooding back.

Further, Steve and Stella realized if they go back to that ranch or others like it, they need to be more aware of the currents in their environment.

THE 'RELATIONSHIP FLU' AND THE CURRENTS IN YOUR ENVIRONMENT

If you were to contract the flu virus, you wouldn't expect to feel its effects immediately. There would be an incubation period before the symptoms showed up. With many disturbances in a relationship, it is difficult to sort out what caused the upset because people look at what just happened and blame the upset on that, rather than looking back at where they went off course 24 to 48 hours before.

It has been our experience that people are rarely, if ever, upset by what has just happened. They are in fact pushed off course or driven out of sync by events that they are, for the most part, unaware of.

We have noticed that when we are riding in a boat, a wave coming from one side or a crosswind can push us off course. But, we don't necessarily notice it until we have gone far enough that the change in direction is apparent. So too, it is with upsetting events. By the time you realize that you are off course, you may have been for some time.

There are people that say or do things that can profoundly affect your relationship and you will not be aware of it, initially. You will only become aware of the effect of their disturbing influence when an upset erupts. At that point you will have already missed what initiated the upset and are likely to assign causality to something or someone in your immediate environment or the last thing that happened. And the way the mind works, if you think you know what upset you, you don't look any further. Just by virtue of spending time with your partner, he or she is likely to become the focal point of upsets because, chances are, he or she will be in your proximity when you realize that you are upset.

TYRONE AND AYESHA

Tyrone had been divorced for three years when he and Ayesha started dating. He had two children from his previous marriage, a boy, age ten and a girl, age seven. Ayesha and Tyrone's relationship grew closer and eventually they set up a home together. His children lived with their mother and came to visit on a regular basis. Tyrone and Ayesha began to notice a pattern in how the two of them related to each other in the days prior to, during and following these visits from the children.

In their normal, day-to-day way of relating, Tyrone and Ayesha were harmonious but in the days just prior to, during and following the kids' visits, they bickered. With coaching, the couple came to expect that as soon as the children's attention turned to coming over to their house, even though Tyrone and Ayesha hadn't spoken with them yet, this was enough to start the dynamic.

At first, it was difficult for the two of them to sort out this situation. To begin with, Tyrone did not want to see that his, 'sweet and innocent' children had brought with them a relationship splitting dynamic. It also didn't initially make sense to the couple that their way of relating could shift even *before* the children arrived. However, by simply observing the repetitive nature of the dynamic, they were able to see the situation without judgment. Once they realized that this change in their way of relating happened with every visit, they could then watch out for it, not judge themselves or the children and then they did not have to automatically bicker.

ＮTIMACY

TRUE PHYSICAL INTIMACY IS AN ACTIVE COMPONENT IN A magical relationship and it is not something to be taken for granted but rather, something to nurture, like a delicate flower. When a couple allows themselves to become vulnerable with each other and uses the opportunity of being sexually expressive to let go of the cares of the day and a chance to communicate their love for one another, sex leaves the realm of being a mere physical act and becomes a sacred expression.

If you want to be able to create the closeness and true intimacy that is possible out of your sexual expression with your partner, it is important to look at the components that have been built into you genetically and culturally, both of which if unexamined, can act as impediments to true well-being.

As little children we have no concept of right and wrong, good

and bad. We are immersed in the culture of our family with its religious and social mores and taboos. By the time you are an adult, chances are that you have conflicting ideas about sexuality. Because there are such pressures not to have sex before you are ready or before you are in a socially, morally acceptable union with a partner, often times individuals absorb the idea that sex is bad, dirty or evil. It is hard to switch from the idea that sex is wrong to allowing yourself to fully enjoy and appreciate this most intimate form of self-expression between two loving individuals. Many times the social conditioning is a silent partner, accompanying you to the bedroom.

We are born into families that have been structured and instructed in the areas of sex and intimacy primarily by religious organizations. Most of us grew up in families where, if sex were mentioned at all, there was a sense that it was not the same as discussing the food on the dinner table or talking about your day. If sex was mentioned, there was some taboo attached to it, whether stated or insinuated. As we move into the teenage years, hormones override inhibitions. As we enter puberty, those hormones are instinctively guiding us for the reproduction and survival of the species. These forces are very strong and can carry us beyond our socialized inhibitions.

Early in a relationship, for many couples we have coached, it is easier to be sexually expressive. At a younger age and with the newness of a relationship, it is enough to override the social and cultural conditioning against sex. Later, however, as hormones slow down and a backlog of unexpressed communications build up, people discover that they have to volitionally generate being physically intimate.

Early in a relationship, even bad breath can be sexy. But, when the fires of passion die down through insensitivity to each other, stresses at work, the incredible demands of parenting, then physical intimacy becomes yet another demand made upon the couple.

Many people don't realize that sex and intimacy become less pleasurable when there are even small, withheld communications. Frequently these withheld communications build into resentments and then sex becomes part of the battleground and the withholding of sex becomes one of those weapons used against one's partner as a revengeful expression for transgressions, real or imagined.

If you are withholding sex from your partner as a form of letting him or her know that you are angry about something, this is one of those times that fully demonstrates being right as opposed to being alive. This form of fighting denies you pleasure, warmth, a feeling of closeness, love, touching and physical intimacy. But, you get to be right that your partner did it wrong and now you are punishing him or her, and also yourself, which leads to feeling less alive.

Before the two of us got together, we each had previous partners. We came to our initial date with a history of things that worked in relationships and things that were problematic for each of us. Very early in our dating we talked about what was important to us regarding sexual intimacy. This, in itself, was a breakthrough because in the past, neither of us had had such a frank conversation with any partner, at any time during a relationship, much less in the very beginning.

To begin with, Shya had recently experienced a long-term relationship where his partner withheld sex. After talking about this, we made each other a promise: If one of us wanted to have sex and said so, then the other would approach the sexual union as if it were his or her idea with the intention of loving the experience. Little did we know that this one agreement would become a stabilizing foundation for our relationship. It allowed us to pull ourselves past the tiredness, distractions and upsets of the day into the realm of intimacy and pleasure. If you truly engage with your partner as if each sexual interlude is your idea and with the intention to love the experience rather than endure it or get it over with, miracles can happen. With this in place, our bedroom and intimate time became a sanctuary from the cares of the world rather than a battleground.

The same evening that we adopted that initial agreement, Ariel made a confession. In her sexual history with other partners, orgasms were elusive. She found that often her partner climaxed and she felt left out or frustrated. So Shya made a promise, "Whenever we have sex, I promise that if you want an orgasm, we will make sure that you have one before we finish."

This allowed Ariel to relax and play and put attention on Shya without having to worry about things getting too carried away so that she was left hanging. Interestingly enough, with the resulting relaxation, trust and ease between us, orgasms became easier and effortless.

Now the agreements we made with each other have faded into the background, but initially, they allowed us to surrender to each other. They were a support structure that helped us pull ourselves past the automatic, 'don't tell me what to do'.

Over the years, the two of us have become more intimate. Intimacy is a natural by-product when we communicate with one another and as we became more trusting and dropped our shields. However, as we opened our hearts, any unaware or insensitive behaviors hurt more acutely. It was important to realize that something that might have been a small transgression at one time took on added weight as we became more vulnerable. Since this is the case, another important tool has been to learn to use the three golden words: I am sorry.

Saying you are sorry, and meaning it, is a miraculous healing tool. We once coached a lady who said she would "rather crawl over ground glass" than tell her husband she was sorry for anything. As soon as she realized that the only thing she had to give up was being right about her point of view, saying she was sorry wiped away years of transgressions, large and small.

The most challenging time to apologize is when you don't feel you have done anything wrong. At these times it is important to rely upon your listening skills. Remember, when you are truly listening, you are listening with the intention of hearing what another has to say from *their* point of view. If you can see your partner's perspective, it is easier to let yourself apologize.

FORGIVENESS

The person that gets hurt most when you don't forgive, when you hold a vendetta, is you because you have to hold on to it. And if you have hateful thoughts, then they run you, they don't help you at all.

If you have a relationship with somebody, without forgiving them for what they did or didn't do, you can't have true intimacy. If you have a list of transgressions, every time you try to be intimate, that list comes between you. So you may have sex, for instance, but it won't be truly nurturing if you're holding onto things that your partner did wrong in the past.

WHAT IT TAKES TO HAVE
THE RELATIONSHIP OF YOUR DREAMS IS FORGIVENESS.
FORGIVENESS INVOLVES GIVING UP THE RIGHT TO PUNISH.
IT IS AS IF YOU FORGIVE A DEBT.
YOU MAKE IT AS THOUGH THE TRANSGRESSION
NEVER HAPPENED IN THE FIRST PLACE.

Please don't misunderstand us. We are not saying that you should turn a blind eye to things that your partner may be doing that do not work for you. Part of what has allowed each of us to keep moving to deeper levels of intimacy has been the willingness to be straightforward with ourselves and with each other about what is acceptable behavior and what is not. However, in any relationship there will be times when each of you will do insensitive things. You can either keep a list of transgressions or you can truly forgive each other and move on.

PRUDISHNESS AND SEXUAL SUPPRESSION

Many people have ideas or fantasies about being sexually free and expressive but, when faced with the reality of the sexual act, often times old conditioning and programming takes over. When you are raised to believe, or *know,* that sex is bad, dirty, immoral or sinful, then those beliefs, if unexamined, will severely erode the possibility of having a rewarding sexual relationship with your partner.

We knew a man who told us that he used to go drinking with his buddies and the conversation would frequently turn to sex and their girlfriends and wives. During these get-togethers, he and his friends would fantasize about what they would like in a woman:

"Oh, I would really love it if my lady was more aggressive. You know, be a tiger in bed."

One night, his wife loosened up and became the tiger he had always wanted. The strangest thing happened. In the midst of their love making, he got scared and started to worry. He had thoughts like: *I wonder where she learned how to do this? I wonder if she was some kind of professional before I married her? What have I gotten myself into?*

Immediately, he found himself getting tight and withdrawn and their lovemaking for that night was over. His judgments of her were so apparent and so suppressive that his wife, never again, allowed herself to be so free and self-expressive.

Another client of ours reported that she once had a partner who was extremely disturbed when she made sounds, of any kind, during intercourse. He was unwilling to look at the possibility that he was prudish and she felt so diminished by his judgments that she quickly ended the relationship.

Again, if you want to have a magical relationship, you must be kind to yourself and to your partner. You must also have the courage to decipher those socially conditioned responses to sex and intimacy so that your prejudices do not dominate your most intimate times together and do not sour what otherwise would be wholesome.

THE ART OF LISTENING

WE TEACH COURSES ALL OVER THE WORLD AND HAVE discovered that whatever the culture, whatever the language, people often don't really, truly listen. Listening is often perceived as a passive act. The two of us have discovered that when 'true listening' is present, satisfying communication is sure to follow. This chapter is devoted to the art of listening. If you discover those things that keep you from listening, you will simultaneously discover many of the things that get in your way in relationships, and in day-to-day interactions. If you learn the art of listening, you will become more effective, productive and satisfied in all aspects of your life.

True listening is not something that we have been taught

growing up in our families, amongst our friends or in school. True listening requires being in the moment. It also requires letting go of your point of view, your thoughts and your agendas. True listening is an art.

Have you ever examined whether or not you are truly listening? Have you identified what inhibits your ability to actually hear what another is saying with the intention of seeing what he or she means from his or her point of view? What we are talking about here is a self-education program.

First you must have the desire to discover how it is that you listen and how it is that you interact with your life from a non-judgmental point of view. It is not about trying to change or fix what you notice in this self-examination of your own behavior patterns. If you just notice how you are relating to your life, that in itself, is enough to complete previously disturbing patterns of behavior. Frequently, there are no other actions needed. This also applies to the way in which you listen, don't listen or distract yourself from listening.

TRUE LISTENING

If a person doesn't feel heard, then frustration builds and misunderstandings are sure to happen. It requires a degree of openness, however, to actually hear what is being said. There are impediments to truly listening to your partner. People frequently are not open to hear simply because they are already involved in a thought or action. We as human beings can only do one thing at a time, if we expect to do it well. Making sure you have your partner's attention is the best way to start when you are saying something of importance.

TRUE COMMUNICATION REQUIRES
THE PERSON LISTENING TO HEAR WHAT IS BEING SAID
FROM THE POINT OF VIEW OF THE PERSON SPEAKING.
THIS IS AN INTENTIONAL UNDERSTANDING
OF THE OTHER'S POINT OF VIEW.

If your partner says, "I really enjoy taking ice cold showers," and you think this point of view is stupid, you will disagree and comment in your head rather than just *hear* what he or she is saying from his or her point of view. However, many of us are so fearful of being manipulated into doing something we don't want to do, that we resist hearing for fear that it will be another request put upon us that we don't want to fulfill.

PRE-OCCUPATION WITH A PROBLEM

If you are pre-occupied with a thought or something you consider problematic, then you can't listen because your mind can only hold one thing at a time. If you are worrying about something, then you won't hear what is being said to you.

The two of us were speaking on the telephone with a friend of ours, Serela. As we spoke, the conversation got more confusing and stilted while she kept talking faster to answer questions we hadn't even asked. Things became rushed, jumbled and frustrating. This was a strange phone call. We wondered what had happened to make Serela, who just the day before had been calm and centered, so distracted and jumpy. We asked some questions in an attempt to solve the puzzling turn of events.

First, we inquired if Serela was sure it was a good time to talk because she seemed rushed. She assured us there was nothing pressing in her schedule, there was plenty of time to chat. So we said she seemed pre-occupied and asked if something had happened in the last day that had upset her. Serela got quiet for a moment and then told us that during the middle of the night, her ex-boyfriend had called. After telling her how mean she was and how much she hurt him and how sad he was because they had broken up, he had hung up on her. All morning Serela had been talking with him in her mind, telling him all the things she didn't have a chance to say. She was arguing with him mentally as she tried to reassure herself she wasn't really a mean person.

When Serela spoke with us, it had been hard for her to really talk and listen because she was already involved in the ongoing conversation in her thoughts. When she simply saw that the phone call from her ex had knocked her off balance, she was restored to herself and suddenly our communications were clear again.

Most of us are unaware when we are actually doing something other than listening. We haven't realized that we are pre-engaged or pre-occupied so that we only partially hear what is being said and that partial hearing is almost always inaccurate.

Have you ever noticed how some people say the same things to you over and over? That is generally because you didn't really hear them the first time. Since listening is an active rather than a passive act that requires your full attention, if you are at all pre-occupied while listening to another, they are left with the feeling that they have not been heard. Which is, in fact, true. How could a baseball player catch a ball if they already have a baseball in their mitt? This is essentially what you are trying to do if you are pre-occupied while listening to another. It is as if you are trying catch a communication while your 'mitt' is already full.

FILLING IN THE BLANKS

As we discussed in earlier chapters, our minds are like computers and they can only operate with what they already know. So, for instance, if you hear a word that you don't already have in your mental data bank, you are likely to fill in the blank with one your logic system assumes is the same or a reasonable facsimile.

Here is an example of how it works:
When we first moved to our home, we were unfamiliar with the area but soon found that one of the towns near where we live is named "Flemington". After we moved in, our friend and real estate broker, Nina, was promoted to a managerial position in a

new real estate office in Flemington – or so we thought. For weeks we drove by her new location and scanned the parking lot, looking for her car. It seemed as though she was never there. Finally we called her and said, "We tried to come by and see you today but you were out. Boy, you must be busy, we keep driving by and your car is never in the lot."

She replied, "What do you mean? I was in all day today."

So we asked if she had a new car, but no, that wasn't the answer. It seems we had misheard when Nina told us she had been promoted. She didn't actually work in Flemington at all. She managed the office in Pennington. Having never heard of Pennington, our minds just filled in the blank.

FILLING IN WITH WHAT YOU EXPECT

When you are in a relationship with someone, after a period of time, you believe that you *know* this person and that you already know what he or she is going to say. When the first few words come out, you assume you know where it is going. So, in your mind, you fill in the blanks with what you expect to hear and stop listening to what your partner is actually saying. You may be right, most of the time. But, there are times when your partner may have been going to say something else and you were not receptive to what he or she wanted to express because you already had the ball in your mitt. Or you may not even hear what is being said because you think you know it already and have already moved on in your thoughts. If so, chances are your partner will feel disregarded.

PROVING YOURSELF RIGHT

At this point, we must talk again about the principle of physics, also the second principle of transformation that says: No two things can occupy the same space at the same time. If your mind is already pre-occupied with what you are intending to say when you get your chance, then there is no possibility that you can actually hear what is being said to you. And that is on the most basic level. If you are defending your point of view, then you won't want to hear what is being said, as in Roger's example of wanting to be paid his 6% right away. When you are defending yourself, your mind will manipulate what is being said so that you can disagree, prove it wrong and prove yourself, or your point of view, right.

Have you ever found yourself finding fault with your partner's use of words or a particular word, rather than allowing yourself to hear the essence of what he or she is saying? Frequently, when people engage in conversation they are trying to prove that what they believe to be true is true. And so, when we listen to another, we are still holding onto our point of view.

IF YOU SIMPLY DROP WHAT YOU HAVE TO SAY AND LISTEN, WHEN YOU RESPOND TO THE PERSON TO WHOM YOU ARE RELATING, YOU MIGHT DISCOVER SOMETHING WHOLLY NEW AND UNEXPECTED TO SAY THAT IS EVEN MORE APPROPRIATE THAN WHAT YOU HAD PLANNED. YOU WILL ALSO FIND THAT IF WHAT YOU HAD TO SAY IS STILL RELEVANT, IT WILL COME BACK ON ITS OWN.

HOW YOU LISTEN HAS BEEN CULTURALLY INFLUENCED

One day, while walking down the street on the Italian Riviera we saw a young girl three or four years old having a conversation with one of her parents. What impressed us most was how she expressed herself with her hands. The cultural way of gesturing in that region is to wave one's hands emphatically as an extension of the words. The girl demonstrated a small version of the gestures going on all around her. She didn't think to learn this way of communicating, it was absorbed along with the culture.

You have also absorbed culturally influenced ways of relating, which include not wanting to appear stupid, being right, and trying to look good. These ways of relating have become filters through which we listen. So listening is not simply an act of hearing what another has to say. Each communication goes through a quick check to see how it might affect our agenda to get ahead, win, be smart or look good.

LISTENING WITH AN AGENDA

A major inhibitor to listening is one's agendas. Wanting something when you talk with another person is not a problem, if you are aware of it. For instance, as a sales person, if you get paid a commission for what you sell, obviously you have a preference that potential customers will purchase something. However, if you push to meet your agenda rather than have attention on taking care of the customers' needs, you are sure to turn people off and lose sales. In effect, going for your agenda often produces the opposite of the desired result.

People are often much more interested in not appearing stupid than they are in actually listening. It is as if it would be bad not to know something and so this agenda blinds the listener. How it blinds listeners is that it doesn't matter what another person is saying to them. Above all else they can't look stupid so they constantly have to be trying to figure out what to say in response.

Please don't misunderstand. There is nothing wrong with having an agenda. If you want a better relationship or more intimacy, for example, that is not a problem. The problem arises when you are unaware of your agendas and you are mechanically driven to fulfill them. If you are aware of the things you want (or don't want) then you can hold these preferences in abeyance and actively listen to what your partner has to say.

BREATHING REALLY HELPS

Sometimes you just have to take a nice deep breath and tell yourself that what your partner has to say isn't going to hurt. It helps to take a deep breath, relax a little bit and listen without defending yourself. The ability to listen without defending is a very powerful tool but it takes self-discipline to allow yourself to actually hear what another is saying without protecting yourself or proving your point of view right.

COMPASSION - COMPASSION - COMPASSION

If your partner is telling you about something you did or didn't do that upset him or her, if you realize that you couldn't have done it any differently than you did, it is possible for you to have compassion for yourself. And when we say compassion for yourself we are talking about a state of grace, of forgiveness. Most of us have the mistaken opinion that we could have lived our lives differently than we did but, if you look back, you will see that everything you did in your life has led you to this point, brought you to where you are now. Though you may think in retrospect that you could have done things another way, when you were actually living through those circumstances, you only did what you could do at that time and you couldn't have done it any differently in reality. Perhaps, *ideally,* you would have done things other than the way you did, but again, that is in retrospect.

To make this point clearer, let's go back to the camera analogy we made earlier. If we were to take a picture of you with a camera and you were sitting down and smiling, could you have in that very same instant of the camera's shutter opening and closing, been standing and frowning? Of course not. Well, two seconds before we took the picture, could you have been different than you were in that moment? The only answer we can come up with is no. Using this camera analogy, if you tease it back in time, you can see how everything that has happened in your life could only have happened the way it did and not the way you think it ought to have happened. This opens the door for the possibility for compassion; compassion for yourself and for others.

In philosophy, there is the concept of determinism vs. free will. By determinism, philosophers mean that your life is predetermined and you really don't have a choice in the way things are. Free will implies that you have total choice in the way things are. What we are saying is that you have no choice in the way things *were*. You may have the idea that the way things were should have, or could have been, different, but the reality is that you have no choice. Things were the way they were. You may have a choice in how things turn out in the future, but the past is already written and you couldn't have done anything differently than the way you did.

THE ONLY THING USEFUL IN THINKING
YOU COULD HAVE DONE THINGS DIFFERENTLY IS
IF YOU WANT TO USE THE PAST TO TORMENT YOURSELF.
WE HAVE FOUND THAT TORMENTING YOURSELF
DOES NOT PRODUCE GREAT RELATIONSHIPS
SO WE SUGGEST THAT YOU DON'T DO THIS.

REINTERPRETING THE PAST

If you accept our premise that 'what is done is done', then the past may be finished but it is still open for interpretation, and this is where many get stuck in tormenting themselves, thereby fettering their abilities to create magical relationships. We would like to offer a story to illustrate another possibility:

There once was an old man who lived in a kingdom and while he was otherwise poor, he was the owner of a magnificent white stallion. One day the King of the land rode through the old man's tiny village and spied the exquisite horse. Being an honorable King, he offered the old man a fortune to purchase such a gallant steed.

The old man thought about the King's handsome proposal and said, "Thank you, Sire, for your generous offer, but I would rather keep my horse."

After the King departed, the villagers surrounded the old man. "Old Man," they said, "What a stupid thing to do. You could have been wealthy beyond your wildest imagination if you had accepted the King's offer!"

To this the old man replied, "Stupid, smart, I don't know. All I know is I still have my horse."

A week or so later, the white stallion broke out of his corral and ran off during the night. The villagers were quick to comment, "Old Man, what a horrible turn of events. Now you have no horse and no wealth either!"

To this the old man replied, "Horrible, wonderful, I don't know. All I know is my stallion is gone."

One week passed and the stallion returned leading a whole heard of wild mares with him. The villagers assembled outside of the old man's corral to admire the mares. "Old Man!" they exclaimed, "What wonderful good fortune. Not only do you have your valuable stallion back but you have the great luck of having a whole heard of mares too!"

Cocking his head, the old man surveyed the stallion and his new mares and replied, "Wonderful, horrible, great luck, bad luck, I don't know. All I know is I have my stallion back and the mares are here, too."

A week later, while trying to break one of the new mares, the old man's only son was bucked off and badly broke both of his legs. The villagers were quick to share their opinion. "Old Man," they said shaking their heads sadly, "What an unfortunate accident. How horrible. If only you had sold the horse then your son would not have broken his legs. Now who will take care of you in your old age?"

The old man replied, "Unfortunate, fortunate, horrible or not, I don't know. All I know is that my son's legs are broken."

A week or two later, the kingdom went to war against a foe with a much stronger army. All of the able bodied young men were conscripted into the army from which they would almost certainly not return...

And so the story goes. You can reinterpret any event in your life to fit your current outlook or agenda. The truth is what happened has happened, and if you see it and let it be, then you can get on with your life. *What?* you might say, *Don't I need to make myself remember and punish myself for wrong doings so that I will never do them again?* No, you don't. If you see something you did or said in error, and actually see it without judging yourself, then you have already learned your lesson. Punishing yourself and feeling badly does not help. If you have truly seen the error of your ways, you never have to repeat them.

THREE GOLDEN WORDS - I AM SORRY!

It doesn't matter how well you communicate, how sensitive you are, how in love and perfectly matched you are with your partner, sooner or later you will do something that blows it. When it happens there is actually a magic wand that can dissolve the hurt and restore your relationship. Truly apologizing can mend a world of hurts. There are some tricks to having it work and other ways of insuring that when you apologize it only inflames the situation more. Here they are:

If you say you are sorry, mean it, really mean it. There is nothing more maddening then having someone say they are sorry just to placate you when they really still think their actions were right. Here is an example. Try saying these words and see which would feel better to hear: "I am sorry *if* I hurt your feelings, or I am sorry *for* hurting your feelings."

If your partner sincerely apologizes you must be prepared to accept it. By the time he or she finally 'admits' the wrongdoing, you may have a backlog of examples of how he or she did the same thing on other occasions. Rubbing a person's nose in it will only reignite the fight and certainly will not make it easy in the future for your partner to apologize again. If you are punished for being truthful, you are much less likely to be honest in the future.

It may be true, in a bigger sense, that what you do does not hurt, disturb or upset your partner, but on a day-to-day level, the truth is that there is plenty you can do that can have damaging effects. Saying you are sorry, and meaning it, only hurts your ego but it can rebuild the bridge between you and another so that you can experience being in love long after the rose of first attraction blooms and fades.

MITCH, THE BURN

LET'S GO BACK NOW TO OUR EVENING SEMINAR, AS TOLD BY Ariel, and continue the investigation into transformation and creating magical relationships.

As the Monday night seminar continued, Shya asked, "Who else has a question?"

The stocky fellow in the back raised his hand. "Well, I guess I do if nobody else is going to talk."

"Go for it," Shya and I responded in unison.

"What's your name?" Shya asked leaning forward and I sensed he already knew the answer.

"Mitch."

"Ahh, I thought it was you. Nice to meet you, Mitch. What can we do for you? What exactly would you like to talk about?"

Mitch had called us earlier in the week to ask what our groups involved. He wanted to know if we could help him with his difficulty in handling his divorce.

"Well, Shya, as I told you on the phone, I am getting a divorce and I am so angry about it. I am not a violent guy or anything, but I have these fantasies of going to where she works and finding her with some guy and picking him up and ripping his lungs out."

The room suddenly got tense. Someone was thinking, *Here is a guy with a real problem. I wonder how they are going to handle it.*

"So, you're angry."

"Yeah!"

"The problem is, you think that your anger is caused by your wife who is divorcing you. You are just angry; the break-up with your spouse is acting like a trigger. Let's see if I can give you an example to make it clearer. Do you know how a bullet works?"

"How?" I could tell that Mitch was mystified by the way the conversation was going. He wasn't sure what a bullet had to do with his current problem.

"A bullet," Shya said "has a projectile in a casing that is backed by combustible material, gun powder and a primer. When the trigger is pulled, the gun's firing pin hits the bullet; there is a chemical reaction that ignites the primer and the gunpowder expands and forces the projectile out through the barrel. If you had a bullet in a casing, minus the gunpowder or the primer, when you pulled the trigger, there would be no reaction. The gun is only loaded when the bullet has a charge. Your wife's leaving you has acted as a trigger, but you are the one pre-charged. Please don't think that I am insensitive to what you are going through. I have gone through a divorce myself and the process was at times agonizing. What I am saying is that your anger isn't caused by anything. In other circumstances, such as driving down the road, when another motorist cuts you off in traffic or doesn't signal a turn, you are likely to get angry too.

We don't recommend that you go searching for an upsetting situation so that you can 'work through' a backlog of emotions, but if a relationship breaks up, or a person who you care about dies and you are angry, hurt or upset, those are the perfect opportunities to allow yourself to feel."

"I know it's not right. I've tried to stop thinking of her and I can't. It only stops when I bury myself in my day, but then at night, thoughts of her are back again."

"I have a question." Shya said, "Are you angry, right now, in this moment?"

"Yeah!"

"Where is this anger located in your body?"

"It's kind of like a burning in my chest," he said, as he placed his hand right over his breastbone and began rubbing it in a circular motion like he had heartburn.

"So Mitch, about this burning sensation in your chest. If it had a color, what color would it be?"

"I don't think it has a color."

"But if it did have a color, what color would it be?"

"Oh, orangey, I guess."

I opened my mouth to say something and Shya turned to look at me. "Are you thinking it is too soon?"

I shook my head no. I knew where Shya's questions were leading even if Mitch didn't, but I also knew one other thing. The outcome of this conversation would totally depend on whether or not Mitch truly wanted to let go of his 'problem' anger.

I was intimately familiar with the series of questions Shya was about to pose. He had posed them to me more than 20 years earlier on our third date.

It had been a beautiful Sunday morning in late August and New York City seemed to be resting up for the week ahead. It was the kind of morning when you could see all the way up and down the avenues and even the bits of paper and debris seemed to glow in the morning sun. What a glorious day for a ride to Jones Beach on the back of Shya's blue Yamaha 650 Special, "Old Blue". We had bundled our towels and sunscreen behind the seat and thus prepared, headed out of town.

It felt like flying. We were dressed in shorts and t-shirts, our heads protected by helmets, and the sun felt good on my skin. What an excellent day to be alive! Even the traffic lights seemed to be going our way.

Shortly after we breezed through the tunnel into Queens, we took an exit and made our way to an open gas station. Pulling up to the pump, Shya stood Old Blue on the kickstand and opened the tank to fill it up. Deciding to stretch my legs, I began to step off when I felt a very sharp searing pain. Jumping with a yelp, I looked down at my left calf at a raw patch with what looked to be a piece of melted skin hanging off. I had placed my leg squarely against the hot muffler. Staring at my injury, I slowly stated the obvious, "I guess I burned my leg."

Just one glance told Shya the whole story and sent him into action.

"Ice!" The station didn't have any so Shya sprinted off in an attempt to locate some. But the commercial neighborhood we were in was resting on Sunday, too. There wasn't even a corner store or local coffee shop open for business. Stuffing a five in the hand of the attendant, we rushed to make our way to Jones Beach, which seemed the closest alternative for ice. The wind on the burn was wicked. The air that had only moments before seemed to spell freedom now brought fire with its touch. The shock of the initial injury having worn off, I was now crying freely as I held Shya tightly around the middle and we sped to the beach.

By the time we pulled into the parking lot, I was beside myself in pain. Pulling up to the curb, Shya hopped off and grabbing our things, he gave me a hand as I limped over to a nearby concession stand where surely they had ice and some cooling relief.

I stood shakily nearby, almost mute with pain, and Shya ran up to the nearest person behind the counter. "Quick, I need some ice. My girlfriend has been badly burned!"

I turned to show her my leg, which by now looked white and

red and raw, thoroughly seared and slightly nauseating to look at. Sometimes when I see a person with a particularly nasty looking abrasion, I get a sensation that shoots into my stomach or groin as I imagine the pain. Had I been a casual observer, I am sure the sight of my leg would have brought a similar rush.

"I'm sorry, we don't have any ice, sir," the salesgirl said in an overly cheery voice. I stared at her. My mouth dropped open. She appeared to be 17 or 18, had brown hair pulled back into a ponytail and I couldn't believe that behind her turned up little nose lurked someone so completely stupid.

"That's not true," Shya practically shouted, trying to contain himself. Even as we were speaking, customers were walking away with giant Cokes that had multitudes of ice cubes protruding from the surface. "Look, she's badly burnt, we need the ice."

"I'm sorry sir, we can't give away any ice. Ice is reserved only for those who buy a soft drink," she said with the same inflection and the same saccharine smile.

Maybe her name is Chatty Cathy, I fleetingly thought. When I was little, my sisters and I had a doll with brown hair that had a tiny record hidden in her body and a string protruding from her neck with a white plastic ring. We would put a finger in the ring and give it a pull and Cathy would say one of eight or nine pre-recorded statements like, "I want to go for a walk," or "May I have a drink of water?" But sometimes the doll would get stuck and say the same sentence over and over no matter how many times you pulled the string.

The girl behind the counter still looked at Shya expectantly as if an order for Cokes or an orange drink would actually be forthcoming when he tired of trying to reason with an automaton. Just as Shya swung his leg up onto the counter to climb over and get the ice himself, Tom the manager, rescued us all.

Pushing his way past the other workers, the slightly pudgy man in his mid-thirties said, "What seems to be the trouble, Marci?"

Her little nose curled up as she prepared to explain, "Well, Tom…"

But Shya didn't want to wait any longer. Still prepared to vault the counter if necessary, he repeated his plea for ice as I showed Tom the burn. In one fluid movement the manager scooped a large cup of ice and said, "Sorry, folks. Be sure to come back if you need more."

As we made our way to a nearby bench, I heard him explain to the girl, "It's OK to give out ice if someone is injured, Marci." Wrapping the cubes in a napkin, I hesitantly pressed the cold to my injury. The touch of the paper was agonizing and I realized I was shaking. As the ice began to melt, dripping down my leg, I finally found some numbing relief.

Eventually, Shya and I shared a plate of greasy french fries and ketchup, and I realized that I wasn't going to get to lie on my towel and sun myself that day. The idea of sand on my calf made me cringe. So we sat at the table, people watching and sipping a giant Coke after all and looking at the tantalizing ocean in the distance as we waited for the chill to take over and quiet the fiery spot on my left calf.

Finally, with the pain mostly under control, we decided to cut our losses and head for home. I refilled my napkin with bits of ice for the ride back to the city and we began to make our way to the parking lot and our trusty steed, Old Blue, who was stoically awaiting our return.

There was only one problem with this plan. By the time we had gotten to the bike, the pain in my leg had reflared ten fold and each stride had become agonizing as the calf muscle flexed and bunched under the wound with each step. It felt as if the skin was drying and cracking. The throbbing that had mostly been held at bay by the icy compresses began to pound in earnest.

I sat down on the curb by the bike, pressed the compress to my leg, laid my head on my knees and began to cry. I could tell my shoulders were lurching up and down with my sobs but they couldn't be controlled any more than the intense throbbing was being controlled by the meager amount of ice I had left in the napkin. Just the idea of wind rushing across the open sore on the way home was enough to cause my sobs to deepen.

Shya sat beside me and took my free hand in his. Gently, his voice came in my ear, "Ariel, let's look at the pain together."

"NO! Don't touch it!" I cried hunching protectively over the leg.

"Ariel," he continued quietly, "I don't want to touch it. Let's just examine the pain. OK?"

Hesitantly, I raised my head. I looked into his intense eyes and slowly nodded as the tears streamed down my face.

"Trust me," he said.

As I gazed into the eyes that were a bluish green flecked with brown, I had no doubt that I could trust this man. There was a calm in him. A steadiness that seemed to translate itself to me. It calmed some of the hysteria of my sobs into sniffles and hiccups but still the tears silently slid down my cheeks because, while I wished I could crawl out of my skin and leave it behind, the pain in my leg was still real and agonizing and no amount of wishing it would be different seemed to change the situation.

"Ready?" he asked. I nodded and so we began. I didn't know at the time that we were going to perform magic. All I knew was that we were going to 'look' at the pain, whatever that meant.

"OK, Ariel. Close your eyes and look at the pain with your mind's eye. If the pain in your calf had a color, what color would it be?"

That was easy. "Fiery red."

"Fine. Now, if it could hold water, how much water would it hold?"

I pictured in a flash the swimming pool from my Alma Mater, Mt. Hood Community College, so I told Shya it was "Olympic Swimming Pool sized."

"OK," he said. "How about now? If it had a shape what shape would it be?"

"Flat, kind of oval with rough and bumpy razor sharp edges sticking out."

"Good Ariel. You are doing just fine. Take a look at the pain now and on a scale of ten, ten being excruciating and zero being no pain, what number does the pain in your leg have now?"

"23!" I knew the number I gave him was off the scale but I didn't care. My leg hurt and it hurt darn bad.

"All right. And if it had a color right now Ariel, what color would it be?"

As I looked, the color had changed. It was now an orangey red with flaring spots of the more intense color and so that is what I reported. As the process continued, Shya kept directing me to look at the shape and color and number and volume of water the spot on my leg held now and now and now. Each moment became separate jewels in time. Not to be gotten away from or ignored or compared to the moment preceding it but individual facets to be investigated and described.

An amazing thing happened. The color changed through yellows to blues and greens, and finally turned white. The volume of water shrank, passing through a kidney-shaped swimming pool size, like the one Mr. Danube, my childhood swimming teacher owned, to a gallon, quart, cup and eventually the volume of water was only to be measured in teaspoons and then drops. Even as the shape shrank to be the size and shape of the head of a pin, so did the numbers of intensity of pain recede to two and then one.

We had done it! We had looked at the pain of the situation squarely in the eye and it had been defeated, disappeared, transformed. I felt a profound sense of relief. And it wasn't just a parlor trick either. Gingerly I got up and walked a bit. The pain had somehow been lifted even more than when I had it totally chilled down with 2 giant soft drink cups worth of ice. And the sensation didn't even really flare up on the ride home, even with the wind wrapping itself around my leg.

Now, sitting in our evening group, I knew as I looked at Mitch that the pain surrounding his divorce, the burn in his heart, seared every bit as much and was every bit as raw as my leg had been. What remained to be seen was if he was willing to let the anger heal.

"Mitch, would it be OK if the anger cleared up?"

"Yeah, Shya, it would feel so good. I have lived with little else for months now."

Shya continued to ask a series of questions similar to the ones he had asked me in the parking lot of Jones Beach that day and as Mitch's colors lightened and the numbers came down in intensity, his face became visibly lighter as well.

Finally, Shya asked one last time, "And if it had a number right now Mitch, what number would it be?"

Mitch opened his mouth to report a number when suddenly he got a surprised look on his face as he looked down at his chest. It reminded me of one of those people you see on TV who looks down to see that the magician has removed their shirt and they didn't feel it go and they have no idea how he did it.

"It's gone!"

There were a few moments of silence at that point. But just a few before Mitch's mind stepped in with the next, obvious question, "What if it comes back later?"

"Mitch, Mitch, Mitch," Shya said with compassion, "Here you are going off into the future again. Do you feel angry right now?"

"No."

"Well then don't worry about it. Did you try to get rid of the anger as we were talking?"

"No," came the reply again. Only this time the reply was a little more mystified as Mitch realized he didn't know how he had gotten to the point where he wasn't throwing himself into an activity and yet still felt calm and centered.

"I wasn't trying to get rid of your anger either. We just looked at it, Mitch. And anything you just look at, rather than resist, loses its hold over you. All I did was to trick you into the moment."

"You have been keeping your anger in place by judging and resisting it. Do you hold anger as a positive thing?" I asked.

"No!" he said with a grin.

"Well, when you judge something as negative, you are not going to want to see it and then it sticks around."

"There is one thing you will have to do in order to not have the anger come back to plague you," Shya continued.

I could tell that Mitch was very interested in what Shya would say next. He wanted some tips, techniques to take away so that if the future showed up like the past, he would be better prepared. He didn't know that Shya wasn't planning to give him a technique. He also didn't know that if you gather a tip for the future so that you can better handle a recurring problem situation, you are destined to repeat the problem. I mean once you get a new set of tools to repair something you think is broken, something inside seems to itch for it to break again just so you can see if they work.

"In order for you to have the anger stop plaguing you, you will have to give up being right — right that she shouldn't have left you, right that you are a victim in this situation. All of that stuff. All you really know for sure is that she is gone and you are getting a divorce."

"Here is an analogy, Mitch: Imagine there are two apartments in life but you can only live in one of them. And in order to live in either one of them, you have to pay rent. The first apartment is the 'Alive' one. In this home you feel alive, have a sense of well-being, are healthy in yourself and have full self-expression. But, in order to live here, you have to give up being right. The second apartment is the 'Right' one. Here you get to be right about your point of view of life and all situations that you face. If someone cuts you off in traffic and you feel ticked off about it, you get to be right that they were jerks to do that and you are right to be angry. But in the 'Right' apartment the rent is giving up feeling in relationship with your environment, being productive and self-expressive. The payment is your aliveness and sense of well-being."

A fellow in the third row spoke up, "You know it's funny. I was thinking about that very thing today. As I was walking to my car, I thought that the cars turning the corner should slow down and let me pass. I mean, what was their hurry? They were only going to turn and get caught by the red light anyway. Once I got in my car and started off to my destination, I wished the pedestrians would hurry up and get out of my way. It seemed so stupid of them not to give me room so that I wouldn't have to come to a stop before turning the corner. To my mind, I'm always in the right and I should have the right of way."

"That's not surprising. The mind acts like a computer. You can transform but your mind doesn't. It still says garbage. It still tells you that you should be angry at the other guy."

"Speaking of angry, how are you now, Mitch?"

"Still at zero Shya, still at zero."

"Are you trying to stay 'at zero', as you put it?"

"Nope. I don't understand it. I just am here."

Ahh, he's getting the hang of it, I thought as I leaned into Shya and he into me. "OK, who else has a question?"

JEWELS

OFTEN TIMES IN A RELATIONSHIP, ONE OR THE OTHER OF THE partners sees something he or she would like to fix in the other. Sometimes it is an annoying habit, but frequently the difficulty arises when your partner is in pain and you can't seem to help him or her. Pushing on your partner, even 'for their own good' can cause a backlash of resistance. Of course resistance energizes the first principle again: What you resist persists and grows stronger.

Here is a story, told from Shya's point of view, which illustrates how, if you try to encourage or push people to do something that you want for them more than they want for themselves, there can be a backlash that you will not like.

Several years ago we lived in Woodstock, NY. One of our favorite pastimes was to visit a store that had a very eclectic bent, as did its owner. His name is Joe and the store's name is "Just Joe". Joe is a sweet, bearded man who has a passion for quality items. We bought our wedding and engagement rings from him because one of the product lines he carries is fine jewelry. We would haunt his store on Saturday mornings because Joe made a wicked double espresso, which went well with his fine Belgian dark chocolates. We would visit on rainy days for the homemade soup du jour and just about any time to look at his antique cars, fantastic bird feeders, oriental porcelain cups and plates, hand woven shawls, kites and high quality cigars from the Canary Islands, etc.

One of the other curiosities that Joe offered was exotic, hand raised tropical birds, parrots and cockatoos. In the midst of the plethora of fun things to look at, touch and buy, stood an enormous wrought iron, handmade birdcage. This palatial cage was inhabited by Jewels, a large sulfur crested cockatoo, a white bird in the parrot family. Jewels and I had a special relationship. Whenever I would come into the store, he would stick his head out of the cage calling to me and raising his crest. The ritual was, as I approached, Jewels would arch his neck, head pointed toward the floor, requesting me to work my fingers between the feathers and give his neck a massaging scratch. Like a dog, when my interest faded for scratching his neck, he would gently nibble my fingers with his beak and bump my hand with his crest, stretching even further between the bars of his cage, encouraging me to continue. Jewels and I were friendly in this manner for several years.

Sometimes when we visited, Jewels would be out of his cage sitting on the counter or riding around on Joe's shoulder. On those occasions, Jewels greeted me and hopped over to my shoulder or hand and extended his neck to be scratched.

One afternoon, Ariel and I visited Joe's and Jewels began his customary straining against the bars of his cage, requesting attention. I said, "Would it be OK if I take Jewels out of his cage?" Joe said, "Sure, go ahead." I scratched Jewels neck in greeting and then I released the latch and pulled open the door. When I reached in and offered him my hand as a perch he did not immediately climb aboard so I nudged his feet with my fingers in hopes of encouraging him to come out and play.

In a flash, Jewels attacked the skin between my thumb and forefinger with his beak. Shocked and already showing blood at the puncture, I yelped and yanked my hand out of the cage. Jewels was still attached. I shook my hand until he fell free and fluttered to the floor. He then proceeded to attack my shoes. I retreated and Jewels began chasing me around the store. Joe called out, "Don't let him catch you. His beak is capable of crushing nuts and can easily pierce your shoe and break your toe."

My relationship with Jewels forever changed in that moment and was never the same thereafter. I realized that for all of Jewels' straining against the bars of his cage, he was indeed at home and felt safe there. It was his comfort zone and I had no right to reach in and try to take him out.

This interaction taught us a valuable lesson, which has supported us in working with people. We have discovered that if people truly want to free themselves from the confining nature of self-defeating habits, negative personal history and the story of their lives, we can assist them in doing that. If, however, people say they want to be free of the limitations that have followed them through life but are actually comfortable in their cages and are unwilling to give that up, then reaching in to take them out becomes a violent act. And they will fight to defend their right to stay in their cages, immersed in the reasons for their inability to be happy, healthy and live in a state of well-being.

We don't mean to give the impression that you shouldn't be willing to give your partner a helping hand. What we are suggesting is that sometimes people say they want help but really don't. We have learned to respect a person's right to stay in his or her cage. It has been our experience that if we exercise patience and keep pointing to the door, then each individual who truly wants to be free will find his or her own way out.

WHEN TO GET OUT

In order to create what is possible in a relationship, it is important to recognize that not all relationships can be magical and not all relationships should continue.

A magical relationship is only magical when it happens effortlessly and naturally. This book is called *Working on Your Relationship Doesn't Work* for a reason. It doesn't work if one or the other partner is clear that he or she no longer wishes to remain in the relationship. If this is the case, then you cannot make this relationship happen.

There are many possible relationships out there for each person but if you stay in one that is dead or in a constant state of battle, mistrust or upset, you will never be able to find one that works.

If you are feeling sorry for yourself in order to punish your partner or as a way of getting his/her attention and that has become your lifestyle, it may be time to dissolve that relationship and discover one that works for you. If you have stopped having fun and life has become an ongoing process of having to manipulate yourself or your partner to keep him or her interested or engaged, it is very likely time to get out of the relationship.

In many relationships, one of the partners recognizes that he or she wants out before the other person comes to this conclusion. It has been our experience that while one individual is the mouthpiece for the relationship, both people have contributed to bringing things to this point. In fact, it has been our experience that both people want out but it is not usually until later that the person who has been 'left' can recognize their part in producing the dissolution of the relationship.

Our workshops tend to attract people who are interested in creating relationship 'magic' in their own lives. The following exchange took place in one such seminar with someone named CJ, about relationships in general and her relationship with her absentee, adulterous husband, in specific. This conversation with CJ revealed so many of the common themes we have seen while working with people about creating and maintaining magical relationships that we have chosen to reprint the conversation in actual transcript format so as to not lose any of the nuances of CJ's challenge nor of our interactions with her. CJ's situation was a classic example of not trusting when to get out.

CJ'S 'SCARF'

CJ: I've always felt like my relationship was going to make me happy and if I could find a relationship that made me happy, then my whole world, my whole life would work out.

Ariel: Your relationship will work out, out of you being fulfilled and happy. If you get two unfulfilled people together, they think that once they mesh up it's going to make a whole. It just makes two incomplete people relating to each other.

Shya: When you first get together with somebody, there are chemicals released in your bodies that mask everything else but your sexual energy. It's so strong that you don't see all the things that you will find wrong with this person. It's like an aphrodisiac, a love potion that's generated in your body. Then it starts to wear off, and the fun and the excitement disappear and there you are with this other person. You're left with you and him. He can never fulfill you.

You see, you're either happy or you're not. A relationship doesn't make you happy, but when it's fresh and new, you've got all these endorphins that are released and you feel better. So you think it is the relationship that did it. You released those feelings, but you attach it to the relationship. The 'high' goes after a while and there you are, stuck with you again.

Ariel: The point where it felt right for Shya and me to get married, was the day I had a direct experience, not conceptually, but a direct experience that I was fine without him. I gave up wishing that he would marry me to fulfill some childhood idea of what I needed to be complete. That evening, Shya started to ask me one question and what came out of his mouth was something else, "Will you marry me?"

This was a surprise to both of us. But it happened out of my already being 'complete'. I hate to use the word complete. The reason I am reluctant to use this word is because I hear a lot of women saying, "I'm very happy to be alone, I'm complete in my aloneness," and we are not using 'complete' in the same way. Their use of the word is usually said having given up that they will ever have anybody. Or, it is a manipulation to get a relationship such as when someone says to herself, *If I try this attitude, then maybe I'll attract someone.*

250

CJ: There's an honesty between you two that is very startling to me because I know that in my relationship, I really get lost. I can't be myself. I feel like if I really show myself, that the person isn't going to like me or there's going to be a judgment and he'll just leave. It's something that I just feel like I can't get over. How do you manage to be so honest?

Ariel: For me, it's taken practice and coming to trust myself. I used to not say a lot of what was going on with me, but that didn't have anything to do with Shya. I held back a lot everywhere. I wasn't even able to recognize what was true for me. I think the first step is to recognize what's true for you.

Shya: It's like that scarf we found for you when we went shopping yesterday, CJ. You know, you've been holding on to a dirty old scarf, because it's a scarf and you need to have one. So what if it isn't the right scarf for you, and isn't a really good match to your complexion and your hair color and the rest of the clothes that you wear. But it's a scarf, you see? That's the way your relationship has been. Yesterday we went to a place with lots of different scarves and tried one on that didn't look that great, tried another one on that looked a little better, but still wasn't quite right, and another one and another, and then we found one that went, "Yes!"

See, you've taken the first man who came along who liked you a bit and said, "Well, he's got to be the one." But it's not a perfect match and it doesn't even feel good, it doesn't feel wonderful. Every time you think of him, you think of your problems.

CJ: That's true.

Shya: So you haven't given yourself the opportunity to meet the right man. You know, Ariel and I had several partners before we met each other. Then when she showed up, it was, "Yes!" We had a date together and I knew she was it. I don't know how I knew, but every cell in my body said yes. Something in me knew. Just like your scarf. Even before you put it on, as soon as you touched it, you knew.

You haven't given yourself the kind of freedom in finding a relationship that you gave yourself to discover the right scarf.

Ariel: Part of it is, if you try on one man and then another man and another man, and it's still not a match, you start thinking there's something wrong with you...like with the scarf, it wasn't the right one, then you tried another and it wasn't the right one, then you tried another and it wasn't and another, and then you started to get despondent thinking you'd never find one that would work for you.

Shya: You make it mean something about you, rather than Mr. Right hasn't shown up yet, and you keep on holding on to a dead relationship that's been dead for years. I wouldn't say that to somebody who had an alive relationship.

CJ: It's like I don't really trust myself.

Shya: Do you trust yourself about the scarf?

CJ: Yes, now I do!

Ariel: Before you found that scarf, you were having a

conversation of *Can I trust myself or not?* It was all a conversation in your mind, because the right one hadn't come along yet. So all the ones that were in front of you didn't look like you, but it looked like they were all the choices we had, and at that point you didn't really trust yourself to be able to see what would be good for you. But when the right one came, all that conversation about trust disappeared.

Shya: As soon as I saw that scarf, I knew it was the right one for you. Everybody knows when it's right. That's why, when you see people in relationships who aren't right for each other, everybody knows that they're not right for each other.

CJ: Somehow, I think that if I work at it, it's going to get better.

Ariel: That reminds me of people who buy shirts that don't look quite right for them and think that if they accessorize it, it will work. So they're constantly manipulating it with this belt and that necklace and *I'll try this scarf over it,* or *How about if I wear these earrings or do my hair just so,* and it still doesn't look right.

Shya: It's easy to see with clothes, because they are inanimate objects that you put around you and your whole way of being changes when you change one object for another object. It's that way with relationships, too. If you're hooked up with a guy and it isn't a perfect fit, it may be okay, but it won't be spectacular. If you trust that the right thing will come along, because it always does, it will. And you don't have to go looking for Mr. Right, he'll show up, and how he'll show up is you'll go out with whoever asks you and then you'll discover if he's the right guy.

You see you don't go out with people who don't fit your pictures. If Ariel didn't go out with me because I was too old for her (when we started dating, she was 24 and I was 41); if she had a rule, *I can't date older men,* then she never would've gone out with me. But you have standards of who you are going to find love with, rather than seeing what the universe provides for you.

CJ: I've been thinking lately, that if I don't stay with Carl there's no one else out there.

Shya: Carl is like your dirty old scarf that doesn't work right and doesn't fit and you don't even like.

Ariel: Part of it is that you think that any man who goes out with you is doing you a favor, rather than recognizing that you have a lot to offer. It goes back to knowing who you are. You settled when you got married. You got married so this person, who you loved, could stay in the country.

Shya: I don't think you should be together. I'll tell you why. You're not together. As you have told us, he's gone to another country maybe four of five thousand miles away from here, and he really doesn't particularly want to be with you. He's got other girlfriends there, and he's got children from other women there. He's has a whole other life there. The only one holding on to your relationship is you.

CJ: I see it now. It's taken me a long time to see that he's really not so interested. That makes me free.

Shya: But you see, you've always been free. You're the one who put the shackles on yourself and blamed it on the marriage. You have the freedom at any time to be with anyone you want to be with. I'm not talking about being sexual, I'm just talking about being with people. Getting nurtured from hanging out with folks. You could also give yourself a relationship, but for it to be successful you have to be yourself first without beating on yourself for being the way you are.

Ariel: Do you have some pictures or connotations around the words 'divorced woman'? That divorcees are failures?

CJ: Yes, absolutely, I'm afraid that I would be a failure. That's true.

Shya: If you were to get divorced, you'd be free. Something very wonderful will happen to you when you have completely cut the ties to a relationship that isn't really a relationship. But for some reason you are holding onto it. It's got to do with your own terror of being alone and the fear that you'll never find the right man.

Ariel: The terror is really not wrapped around men, its just terror. That same terror, to a lesser degree, came up every time we took a scarf from around your neck and it looked like there would never be that right one. And part of your freedom lies in experiencing what is there to be experienced and that includes the terror. When you allow yourself to experience being terrified, the terror will dissolve.

DISCOVERING
WHAT YOU TRULY WANT

OFTEN TIMES PEOPLE ARE CONFUSED AS TO WHETHER OR NOT TO stay in a relationship. The most common response to this indecision is to step back, take your hands off the wheel and your foot off the gas. Usually people want to judge, evaluate and think about the situation.

Stepping back will never answer your question. Oh, you will come up with an answer but it will be generated from your thought processes and the story of your life.

If you want to know if you are in the 'right' relationship or on the 'right' track, engage! Not just with your partner but in all aspects of your life. In order to have magical relationships, it requires an active engagement with what is going on in your life right now.

SURRENDERING TO YOUR LIFE IS THE KEY

As we mentioned earlier, when you surrender you don't lose anything. Surrendering allows you to assume responsibility for your life. It is about operating as though the circumstances of your life are truly your choice and you are choosing what you have, not thinking about your preferences. It is operating as though you really want to do whatever it is that your life presents you with, rather than victimize yourself with your life circumstances.

For most of us, however, there is inertia; it's almost as if certain aspects of our lives are covered in molasses. There are years of disappointments that make it appear that it is not worth it to try, that it is not worth it to go for it. What it takes to get through the inertia is to get engaged with totality. If you are going 100%, if you are engaged in your life with totality, your truth becomes apparent, but not as an intellectual exercise. Your truth will reveal itself to you more as an 'of course'.

A lot of the resistance you will experience in going for your life with totality is based on an idea of your own inadequacies put together by an earlier version of yourself, a much earlier version. Again, since the mind is a recording machine of previous conversations regarding the events of our lives, it holds onto old concepts as if they are still fresh and new. When we were very young, our motor skills and coordination were nowhere near what they are as adults, yet a lot of our beliefs and conversations about what we are capable of and what we can or cannot do come from decisions that were formed long before puberty. Ideas that we have of our own desirability, attractiveness and worth were put in place long before the current version of us came to be.

This being the case, apparently there is nothing you can do except continue to have the same conversations you have had in the past. Ahh, but there is something called transformation. Transformation is discovering how to access and live in the moment. If you get into this current moment and notice old mechanical behaviors as they show up, the noticing of them and the noticing of your own considerations about who you are and what you are capable of will dissolve these behaviors and will allow you the freedom to discover and be yourself.

ENTHUSIASM = LIFE

What you need to generate the energy to pull yourself into your life and into the moment is enthusiasm. Many of us don't have that enthusiasm to start with. We are swayed by our thoughts that repeat our inadequacies so that we don't even bother trying. It is said that the longest journeys start with a single step. You have got to begin. How does one become enthusiastic? Well, most people are looking for something that is worthy of pouring their heart, soul and passion into. Fear not. You don't have to look far. Glance around. Where are you in this moment? It doesn't matter. You can start to generate the enthusiasm you naturally have for living now, in this moment. In fact, that is the only time there is. You don't have to wait for the circumstances to line up to a more favorable position. You have the perfect circumstances for transformation, right now.

Look around your house, your apartment, wherever you are. There are things that you have been avoiding completing forever. See what they are and do them. Too tall an order? OK, start with one. Any one. Completion of projects, in fact completion of any kind, returns energy to you. Wash the dishes, make your bed, make that call, run that errand. Start. Starting anything gives you power. Notice when your thoughts say I can't do it, I am not good enough, I will never be able to get this done and do it anyway. That is the beginning. That is the beginning of reclaiming your life. Feel your energy rush back into you. Feel yourself come alive. It doesn't have to be a monumental project. Start with a burned out light bulb or dusty area you have been skirting around for weeks.

261

LIFE IS AN EXCITING ADVENTURE.
IF IT DOESN'T APPEAR THAT WAY TO YOU,
THEN THERE IS SOMETHING THAT YOU ARE
PREOCCUPIED WITH, OTHER THAN YOUR LIFE;
PROBABLY YOUR THOUGHTS ABOUT YOUR LIFE.
SEE IF YOU CAN NOTICE THAT YOUR THOUGHTS ARE
JUST THOUGHTS AND ARE NOT REALITY.

The two of us are firm believers in the 'fake-it until you make-it' school of life. If you can't find enthusiasm for your relationship right now, fake it! Faking it will lend you the ability to go with totality and before you know it, you won't be faking it anymore or you will be energized to recognize actions that need to be taken.

E X E R C I S E S

DISCOVERING WHAT YOU TRULY WANT

1. Play a game. When you are washing the dishes or experiencing difficulty communicating, for example, quietly say to yourself, ...*and this is what I want.*

   If you are having fun say, ...*and this is what I want.*
   If you are upset or angry say, ...*and this is what I want.*
   If you think this is a stupid game, say to yourself, ...*and this is what I want.*

2. Find something simple to complete and complete it. (Feel free to repeat!)

FUN IS NOT
A FOUR LETTER WORD

OH, THE PRESSURE! MEN AND WOMEN ARE TRYING TO FIND "THE One." When looking for a potential mate, the urge to get in there and make it work is a driving force. People are so busy looking for someone who is relationship material and finding Mr. or Ms. Right that they forget to have fun. In fact, dating to have fun is thought of as frivolous or secretly held as downright immoral. If you are going out to enjoy yourself and have fun, rather than finding a marriageable mate, it is generally viewed as a big taboo.

Not true of me! you might say. *I think having fun is really fine and a great idea.*

OK, fill in the blank: A woman who has four dates with different guys in one week is a _____.

Or, fill in the blank: A fellow who is dating four different women is a _____.

Of course, some of you might fill in the blank with the idea that he or she is 'lucky', but is that really the truth? Have you ever found it difficult to date, even casually, more than one person at a time? Have you ever had only one date with someone and then spent a lot of time thinking about him or her to the exclusion of all others? Have you ever passed up going out because you are waiting, hoping for that fantasy phone call or email that never comes? Or, have you pined for someone who lives in another city or country, knowing full well that you have no intention of moving and neither does he or she?

Over the years, we have seen both men and women immediately pin their hopes on one person to the exclusion of all others. Take, for instance, Jessica:

Jessica started trading emails with Bill, a man from an online dating service. He seemed so nice that she didn't answer the other emails from prospective suitors because hopefully, this fellow would prove to be her boyfriend. She thought about him a lot and looked forward to seeing what other messages would come. Eventually they talked and finally they had a date, and then two.

Jessica found out that she and Bill had no chemistry in person. In fact, his views in real life were different than what he had portrayed in writing and his judgments of her were offensive. Since Jessica had let all of the other potentials fade away, now she had to start all over. But she felt discouraged, decided to take a break from online dating and before she knew it, months had gone by without going out. Jessica began to think of herself as simply unattractive. Once you lose your momentum, it is hard to regain it.

What if you just started to go out for fun? See if you can include the societal programming for finding a mate and then simply let yourself enjoy people, lots of people. The best place to start is everywhere! If you begin to let yourself have fun with the person you buy your coffee from in the morning or the ticket seller at the movies or the person in the checkout line, you will begin to relax and be more yourself. Being yourself is really attractive.

Who are you more likely to be interested in:

Someone who is enjoying himself or herself and taking pleasure in the moment or someone who is trying to fulfill an agenda?

A friend of ours recently told us of a blind date she had with a man, which started out light-hearted enough, but by the end of that first evening, he started talking about the two of them getting married. It totally turned her off. Obviously, relationship isn't something you can force.

If you recognize and sidestep the trap of trying to achieve a relationship, you may discover yourself having so much fun with someone that a relationship simply and beautifully happens.

Some of you may be reading this and thinking, *Thank goodness I have found my partner and I don't have to worry about dating anymore.* If this is true for you, then here is a question: What have the two of you done for fun lately?

STARTING OVER

HAVE YOU EVER FOUND YOURSELF IN ONE OF THOSE MOODS where no matter what your partner says or does, it is all fodder for the fight? Where you are angry, disturbed and nothing he or she says or does is right or good enough to relieve your sense of aggravation?

We recently met a couple involved in one of these altered states of consciousness. They came to speak to us about their relationship and how, no matter what they did, it always ended in an upset and distress and their fight never seemed to completely resolve. Oh sure, it abated from time to time, but the embers of disagreement were always just below a thin skin, ready to erupt at any time.

The funny thing about it was, they were both right, from their individual points of view. From his point of view, "She would always..." and from her point of view, he was wrong and all of her friends agreed with her take of the situation. This couple had a list of grievances, which dated back to early in their relationship. These were past events over which the two of them continued to disagree.

Hal and Mary had in their relationship fundamental behavior patterns that we have seen in other intimate relationships where nothing seems to resolve. No matter how much they had tried to change or fix the situation, it continued to stay the same or got worse. So they came to us, looking at whether or not they should remain together. Their situation was further complicated by the fact that they had a 16-month-old child together. By now, the sense of intimacy between the two of them had completely eroded and while they were very devoted to their daughter, she had become the focal point for many of their fights.

The real problem was that Mary and Hal, for all of their strife, were obviously still in love. They just couldn't find a way to sidestep the old grievances that kept resurfacing, incendiary mechanical behaviors, that set them battling against their will.

Our usual approach is to find out where it all started and what happened that initiated the fight but, when asked what caused this behavior in the first place, both Hal and Mary each had their reasons for what the other did or didn't do that created the situation and both of them were 'right' from their points of view. Apparently, we had a stalemate or deadlock. No matter what we came up with, each person felt justified in their experience that the other was the cause of their stress, upset and dissatisfaction. This is normal for most relationships that are in trouble.

In situations like the one with Hal and Mary, where they have been together several years, the starting point of the disagreement is obscured forever. So what do you do to alleviate the pain when you are locked in a habituated way of relating that seems to have no beginning and no end and keeps accelerating in its frequency, intensity and duration?

At some point, the reasons why you are upset become irrelevant because everything becomes grounds for the disturbance. It has been unresolved for so long that there is no way to go back and fix all of the grievances and transgressions.

So what do you do then? You can leave each other, which is the end result that a lot of loving relationships devolve into…it is called divorce. You can punish each other perpetually and live a life of complaint and pain. Or, you can start over.

Here is how we have done it. There have been times in our relationship when we have found ourselves fighting and we could not find a way out of the disagreement in which we were locked. Finally, we came up with a device that allowed us to stop fighting. This is what happened:

One day, we were driving into New York City and for whatever the reason, we were deeply engaged in disagreeing with each other. It escalated and it was like a sore tooth that you worry with your tongue; we couldn't seem to leave it alone. Our silences were noisy, very noisy. And, each of us was certain that we were right in our own point of view and that the other was simply wrong. We each felt picked on and misunderstood. It didn't feel good, but there didn't seem to be a way to resolve the conflict. Finally, we came up with the idea of starting over. We picked out an overpass ahead on the highway and said, "When we go under that overpass, it is *over.*" This meant that as soon as our car passed that spot we were going to operate as if this disagreeable conversation had never taken place. So on we drove. It took discipline at first to resist the temptation of thinking about the altercation that had just happened but we kept bringing our thoughts and conversation to current things such as what we could see out of the window and our plans for the day rather than rehashing the past.

We can't remember now what our fight was about. It seemed so important at the time, but now the details have faded into obscurity. We knew that the fight could fade away for Hal and Mary too, if given a chance, and so we suggested to them starting over. We warned them it would be challenging to not keep habitually going back to past gripes but they grew excited and intrigued at the idea.

That night, Hal and Mary had a date. They had not been on a real, live date since before their child was born.

SOMEDAY

THERE ARE LOTS OF 'SOMEDAY' THOUGHTS THAT WILL undermine your relationship:

> Someday, things will be better.
>
> Someday, I will stop behaving this way.
>
> Someday, I will get over these mechanical behaviors.
>
> Someday, he (or she) will change.
>
> Someday, when we get married, we will be happier.
>
> Someday…

Over the course of reading this book you have seen yourself and how you mechanically relate. Your eyes have opened to hidden agendas, prejudices and many ways, large and small, that you have gotten in your own way when creating the relationship of your dreams. And now, if you are like most people, you will secretly have the new agenda to eradicate these 'negative' things from your life. You are going to get past your prejudices, sidestep your petty thoughts and the urge to fight with your partner and move on to a healthier, happier way of relating.

Well, guess what? That is *change,* not transformation. You can transform but the mechanics of your mind don't. When you discover that this moment is all that there is and that some future, fantasy someday is not going to save you, then instantaneously you are healthier and happier but, you don't have to change you, your partner or your circumstances first.

The moment is like a movie and the soundtrack is laid alongside. Your soundtrack may be saying pleasant things or it may be complaining. The mind is a machine and expecting the way it works to change, will only set you up to be upset and disappointed. When the circumstances of your life become stressful enough, challenging enough or when there are strong currents in your environment that are working on you, you can expect that old familiar ways of relating will resurface.

When a tree is cut down, you can see the rings that were formed during each year of growth. They represent the times of plenty of sun and rain and the lean years, too. Part of the beauty in a hardwood floor or table, for example, is the grain of the wood. Well, your mechanical behaviors are like wood, they are ingrained. If you work on yourself, whittling away and try and sand off the grain, you have none of you left. As we said in *The One Who Listens* chapter, where Ariel watched the tape loop of the time lapse photography where the red rose sprouted, grew and blossomed, your mechanical behaviors were pre-set in another time, in another place, by an earlier version of yourself and it cannot be changed.

274

PLENTY OF PEOPLE HAVE COME TO US DISCOURAGED
BECAUSE THEY HAVE LOST THEIR WAY
AND HAVE STOPPED FEELING TRANSFORMED.
YOU WILL, AT TIMES, LIVE IN THE MOMENT
AND THEN THERE ARE TIMES WHEN YOUR MECHANICS
WILL TAKE OVER AND YOU WILL BE REPEATING
OLD BEHAVIORS FROM THE PAST. EXPECT IT!
IF YOU EXPECT TO HAVE YOUR EARLIER WAYS OF RELATING
WITH YOU FOR THE REST OF YOUR LIFE
THEN YOU ARE MUCH LESS LIKELY TO BE
HARD ON YOURSELF OR RESIST THEM WHEN THEY RESURFACE.
IF YOU RESIST OLD MECHANICAL WAYS OF RELATING,
THEN OF COURSE THEY PERSIST AND GROW STRONGER.

A friend of ours, James, recently told us that he and his wife started a heated argument immediately following his family visiting the two of them. Within 10 minutes, James realized, *This is not our normal way of relating. We must have gotten knocked off balance somewhere in our interactions with my family.*

James said it was akin to suddenly being on a carnival ride through an old familiar house of horrors. But, with awareness, he and his wife realized that the fight wasn't serious, wasn't their truth and it was as if they were able to jump off the bumpy ride together and land on their feet. In the past, fights like this had gone on for days or months with lots of self-recrimination, bruised feelings and recovery time. Because James and his wife did not judge themselves for falling back into an old mechanical way of relating, the situation instantaneously transformed.

Transformation is a skill-set, and like any other skill, you get better over time as you practice. This is one of the biggest paradoxes in our approach.

TRANSFORMATION IS INSTANTANEOUS
YET THE EFFECTS ARE CUMULATIVE OVER TIME.

276

SOMEDAY, WHEN I FIX THIS ONE THING, THEN I WILL BE HAPPY

There was a man who was taking a trip by train and he booked the top berth in a sleeping car for the night. Just as he was drifting off to sleep, he heard the man in the berth below him begin to moan, "Oh, I am so thirsty. I am *so* thirsty!" After realizing that the other fellow was going to continue complaining and that he would not be able to sleep, the man sat up, climbed down from his berth and fetched the traveler on the lower level a glass of water. Satisfied that he had solved the situation, the man returned to the upper bunk and stretched out once more. Just as he was drifting off to sleep again, he heard the man in the berth below him say, "Oh, I was so thirsty. I *was so* thirsty!"

If you think that when the thing you are complaining about gets handled, then you will be happy, you are setting yourself up for a big disappointment. Complaining is a habit. Complaining just energizes the part of you that complains.

SOMEDAY, I WILL HAVE A BETTER RELATIONSHIP

The relationship you currently have is the best that is possible for you, in this moment. If you are currently single, then the relationship you have with yourself is the best it could possibly be in this moment and you can only have what you have. (Second principle.)

In order to create a magical relationship, you have to be willing to be yourself, now, exactly as you are and exactly as you are not, rather than waiting around for some new, improved version. If you are trying to improve yourself, then that is a long and arduous road. And perhaps you will eventually improve... incrementally...in certain limited areas and not in others.

When you have the courage to see yourself honestly, and do not judge yourself for what you see, then your life will transform and your relationships will transform along with it. Transformation is like the philosopher's stone in alchemy that was purported to turn base metals into gold. Transformation takes an ordinary, mundane relationship and turns it into a magical one.

ACKNOWLEDGMENTS

Our sincere thanks to the Mastery of Self Expression Program participants, both in the United States and in Germany, for your courage, support and partnership. You are an inspiration.

We specifically want to thank all those who have read and helped edit the manuscript in all its incarnations. You have been so generous with your time, energy, expertise and commitment to excellence.

We sincerely appreciate Amy Beth Gideon for so graciously letting us reprint her article, Why Do I Worry About Silly, Silly Things?! Also, this project could not have been completed so well or so elegantly without the photos of Bill Sayler and meticulous and talented work of Danielle Linares, our graphic designer.

It was a baffling exercise for the two of us when we attempted to thank our support team in terms of their contribution to this project. So, we have fallen back on the time-tested system of listing names alphabetically.

Special thanks also goes to:

Josh Blau	Judy Mines
Laura Blau	Isabelle Monaco
Mike Donlon	Tony Monaco
Sue Donlon	Josh Pais
Paul English	Lenore Pemberton
Bob Finnen	Eric Pomert
Stephanie Finnen	Valerie Pomert
Marie Forleo	Charlotte Sayler
Andy Gideon	Christina Sayler
Roderick Hill	Dave Stern
Ellen Jackson	Anne Vince
Mac Jackson	Elizabeth Caitlin Ward
Dirk Keysser	

WHAT PEOPLE ARE SAYING ABOUT THE KANES' SEMINARS AND CONSULTING SESSIONS

What we love about the Kanes' workshops is that their approach is geared as much for couples whose relationships are solid and working well, as for couples who are struggling with particular issues. We are regularly amazed at how a great relationship can get better. We use the Kanes as catalysts to further our own journey of self-discovery, intimacy, partnership, communication and fun. We've been together for eight years, married for six, and doing these workshops has had a tremendously positive impact on the quality of our relationship.

Bob and Stephanie Finnen

We know of no better personal coaches in the art of relationship than Ariel and Shya Kane. Thanks to the clear and gentle guidance we've gotten from attending their workshops, our relationship is far less about trying to get someplace 'better' and much more about being a team that makes a difference in peoples' lives. Through the practice of living in the moment, the mental clutter of our lives has dramatically cleared away, leaving us to be ourselves and greet each day with a continually renewed gusto. The Kanes have also taught us how to truly listen – to our own truth, intuition and to each other as well.

We met in one of Ariel and Shya's weekend workshops over two years ago and have since gotten married. Planning a wedding can be stressful and time-consuming. Ariel and Shya's coaching was instrumental in making our wedding an easy, manageable project that came together beautifully without disrupting our day-to-day lives. Without rules or fix-it techniques, Ariel and Shya's courses have become a key support structure in allowing our love for each other to deepen and flourish. Ariel and Shya Kane have been a gift in our lives. They have helped us recognize the miracles that happen in our lives every day.

Valerie and Eric Pomert
Nutley, NJ

My husband Bill and I have been married for 42 years and counting. About eight years ago we went to one of the Kanes' two week winter seminars on 'living in the moment'.

At that time and for almost all of our relationship we related in a way I would describe as putting up with each other and hating it. We both were dissatisfied but were not going to do anything about changing things because that would have been just too scary to contemplate. It would mean financial decisions and admitting we had failed. It was easier to just live with things as they were. After all, I couldn't do any better anyway!

We thought this was as good as it could be in a relationship. We were just plodding along waiting for our lives to be just a little better or waiting for that big break Bill would get someday with his art career and then everything would turn out all right. Maybe we could earn a little more money and then things would be better. Just better!

I can remember being angry most of the time. Everything and every decision, every move was his fault if it didn't turn out. If it turned out at all it had to do with luck. My life looked the way it did because he wasn't this or he didn't do that. I had minimal to no responsibility in how the circumstances in my life showed up. We would fight and bicker all the time. I would get really angry, he would sulk and be silent, take himself away for days. I also resented that he never advanced in his career. I had fantasized he would someday become a well-known exhibiting artist and then I could vicariously be important and famous as the dutiful wife of this 'genius'!

After being in the seminar for just a short time I came to see how I had totally blamed all the negative circumstances in my life on him. I had taken myself out of the equation. It was his fault and I gathered agreement from my family and friends to justify the way I saw it. I actually saw that the way we were relating effected how effective he was. I also experienced myself as an independent being that was totally capable and responsible for the way my life was and the circumstances in it. Out of being in the workshop we got to see how much we indeed did love each other. We were in love and had the possibility in each moment to interact with each other in a way that was new and fresh. Our lives have become about being a team, not a competition for who is right and who is wrong. Our lives have become an exciting adventure.

Oh, recently Bill has had two successful exhibits at a gallery, sold work and has become a tenured professor at the largest art school in the world. We have more money than we ever dreamed was possible. I am a Dental Hygienist and have two other businesses, both of which are very successful. In addition, our relationship to our daughter is beyond what we ever could have imagined was possible.

Ariel and Shya Kane's work definitely works. We are the living, breathing examples of what is possible out of 'living in the moment' and we love every moment of it.

Charlotte Sayler
Brooklyn, NY

Before attending the Kanes' Magical Relationships seminar you could have considered our relationship to be a good one, but there was always an underlying current of disagreements and bickering that showed up in our communication and how we related to one another. An unspoken grudge existed between us where each of us thought we were right and the other was wrong. While we knew we were the one for each other, we really hadn't known that there was another way of relating, one of partnership, before meeting the Kanes. In a light and easy way, the Kanes provide the keys to unlock the door for truly magically relationships with yourself and others, where life becomes fun, alive and satisfying. After attending the Kanes' seminar, we now see a choice in how we relate to each other. We are not on automatic mode for fighting. We now have the eyes to see our partner not as the same old person with our past history, but as a true friend in our adventures of a lifetime together. We recently celebrated our fifth wedding anniversary, which was a joyous occasion for us as well as everyone around us! We whole-heartedly recommend the Kanes' Magical Relationships seminar.

Sincerely,
Susan Donlon, Vice President Bear Stearns & Co. Inc.
Mike Donlon, New York City Fire Department Captain

OTHER OFFERINGS BY THE KANES

INSTANTANEOUS TRANSFORMATION EVENINGS

These evenings are exciting explorations which open the door to living in the moment. Each session is a unique impromptu event formed by the interests and questions of those who attend. Not just an introduction to the work of Ariel and Shya Kane, they are actual opportunities for people to discover their ability to relate effectively and experience satisfaction in all areas of their lives.

MAGICAL RELATIONSHIPS: HOW TO GET 'EM, HOW TO HAVE 'EM & HOW TO KEEP 'EM

Since their first date in 1982 and subsequent marriage in 1984, Ariel and Shya have discovered that there are specific keys to finding a relationship, and keeping it alive, exciting and new. Whether you are searching for someone or already have found the person of your dreams, this workshop reveals how to truly have Magical Relationships.

CREATIVITY & INTUITION

Increasingly individuals are discovering the power and importance intuitive hunches play in their ability to be creative, successful and satisfied in their lives. In a light and fun way, this workshop will allow you to hone this intuitive skill-set into a fine instrument that can be used to thoroughly enhance your day-to-day experience of living. It will include a series of experiments and exercises designed to allow you to discover and trust your own natural abilities to access and utilize your intuition and creativity.

TRANSFORMATIONAL TIME AND PROJECT MANAGEMENT

In this course, participants learn to interact in a way that allows for the effective, easy, and effortless completion of projects and tasks. This fun and lively interactive seminar inspires people to see projects in a whole new way. This technique of managing time eliminates stress and feeling 'overwhelmed' becomes a thing of the past.

TRANSFORMATION IN THE WORKPLACE: A COMMUNICATION SEMINAR

This seminar provides an environment in which participants can explore various aspects of their communications and behavior and the impact they may unknowingly have on others in their work environment. In a loosely structured format, designed to allow one to discover the nuances of true communication, this course acts as a non-judgmental laboratory environment which reveals and dissolves those unaware, reflexive behaviors that are counter-productive in an office environment. Transformation in the Workplace is appropriate for people of all professions and is specifically geared towards those companies and individuals who want to operate at peak efficiency and who desire to have work be a highly satisfying experience.

Some of the areas in which previous participants have reported dramatic results:
- An increased ability to listen to clients and respond to their needs
- Increased productivity
- Increased sales
- Greater job satisfaction
- Greater rapport with managers, co-workers and/or staff
- Less job related stress
- Fewer sick days
- Greater ease in dealing with 'problem' situations
- The job becomes a place to express oneself

INSTANTANEOUS TRANSFORMATION
TWO AND A HALF DAY WORKSHOPS

In this exciting in-depth exploration, participants will have the opportunity to have a direct experience of Instantaneous Transformation. Rather than teach techniques, the Kanes empower participants to get into the moment and reclaim their natural ability to access this state at will.

This workshop is designed to reveal and dissolve the mechanical behaviors and barriers which limit our lives and keep us stuck in our memories of the past or our plans for the future. In this course, participants can discover fulfillment in their lives without working on their 'problems'. Through light and playful exercises and group discussions the Kanes act as catalytic agents in facilitating people's discovery of their own truths.

At the end of the workshop participants bring home a deeper awareness, an expanded sense of self, a heightened sense of self worth, a less stressful attitude toward previously distressing situations, and a strengthened ability to be present in the moment – regardless of the circumstances. As a result, they discover a more honest, true and natural way of being that allows them to be increasingly effective, and satisfied, in all aspects of their lives.

THE ART OF BEING A HEALER

All of us are healers. Regardless of our roles in life, or our vocations, we all have the ability to heal ourselves and to be a healing presence for those around us. This course is not about learning another technique. It is about discovering the healer that dwells within each of us so that we can access that place at will. Participants discover the possibility of healing themselves and others with a beauty and simplicity that far surpasses what we know healing to be.

THE FREEDOM TO BREATHE

This course is designed for people who want to dissolve the unconscious restrictions which limit their lives. Using breath as a tool, it is a gentle entry into the moment which can release past trauma, both emotional and physical, and result in a dramatically expanded sense of oneself.

THE ART OF RELATING

Imagine what it would be like to be able to relate well, day in and day out, not just when the circumstances happen to be easy. The Kanes have discovered the secrets to having relationships be fresh, loving and alive. After more than 20 years together, people still ask them if they are newlyweds. Ariel and Shya invite you to join them as they share the key elements that bring relationships out of the realm of the ordinary and mundane and into the realm of the miraculous. This workshop will empower you to have nurturing and fulfilling relationships in all areas of your life. In *The Art of Relating,* you will rediscover your ability to create intimate, exciting and profound relationships – including the one with yourself.

MONEY, SUCCESS & HAPPINESS: THE ART OF BEING WEALTHY

When you discover how to live in the moment, money, success and happiness are natural expressions of your life rather than things to strive for. This course will allow you to discover how to have a wealthy and satisfying life.

Internationally acclaimed seminar leaders, business consultants and authors, Ariel and Shya Kane, are expert guides who, with great skill and humor, bring participants through the swamp of the mind into the clarity and brilliance of the moment. By using the Kanes' Instantaneous Transformation technology, thousands worldwide have learned how to easily have richer and more fulfilling lives.

Can you imagine what it would be like to live your life in a way that you stopped second-guessing yourself? Where you live your life directly rather than think about whether you should or shouldn't or should have or shouldn't have? Where you stop going for other people's approval or even your own and lived your life from your truth rather than trying to fit in?

This workshop is an exciting exploration, which opens the door to living in the moment. Through discussions and laughter you will discover how to: be satisfied in all areas of your life; relate in a more honest and natural way; remain centered during life's challenges; eliminate stress and dissolve mechanical behaviors that rob you of your spontaneity and creativity. As a result you will take back control of your own life. During a portion of the course you will use breath as a tool to gently enter into the moment, which can release past trauma, both emotional and physical, and result in a dramatically expanded sense of oneself.

This course is specifically designed to allow you to reconnect with your natural ability to live your life directly in the moment rather than second-guessing or complaining to yourself about your choices.

A must for every seeker of the truth, this weekend workshop is an exciting adventure, which will allow you to discover how to easily and effortlessly live in the moment and not in your thoughts.

EXECUTIVE CONSULTING

Individual consulting is available for those executives interested in achieving revolutionary increases in productivity, income, rapport and job satisfaction.

SEMINARS FOR COMPANIES

The Kanes tailor private seminars to meet the needs of individual organizations.

PRIVATE SESSIONS

The Kanes meet with individuals and couples in person and by phone.

SEMINARS IN YOUR AREA...

If you want to know the Kanes' current schedule of events,

check their website at:
    http://www.ask-inc.com

or write to them at:
    ASK Productions, Inc.
    208 East 51st Street, PMB 137
    New York, NY 10022-6500

or email them at:
    kanes@ask-inc.com

The Kanes do not target specific areas in which to lead workshops. They only bring their technology to those people who request it. If there is not an event scheduled in your area and you are interested in having Instantaneous Transformation where you live and work, contact them...they listen.

Working on Yourself Doesn't Work
A Book About Instantaneous Transformation
(ISBN: 1-888043-04-0) $12.95

WORKING ON YOURSELF DOESN'T WORK reveals a revolutionary new approach that will allow you to reach a state of awareness and 'centeredness' that in the past was rarely, if ever, achieved. This book contains the keys to transform your life. It is a radical departure from the concept of working on yourself to bring about change. There are no gimmicks to learn, no rules to live by, or pre-set paths to follow. The Kanes' Instantaneous Transformation technology is about a change of states, a shifting of realities — which will produce a quantum shift in your life.

Working on Yourself Doesn't Work
A Book on CD About Instantaneous Transformation
2 hrs 1 min   (ISBN: 1-888043-11-3) $19.95

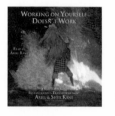

The Art of Living in the Moment
A Bilingual Adventure in Transformation
2 hrs 14 min   (ISBN: 1-888043-12-1) $19.95

Join the Kanes and Hamburg, Germany course participants in this exciting two CD set as they have a lively, practical, and down-to-earth conversation about the art of living in the moment. (These evenings were recorded with live translation into German.)

By listening to this audio program you will learn:
*   The keys to living in the moment and having a magnificent life
*   The Principles of Transformation and how they can help you reconnect with your creativity, spontaneity and excitement
*   How to remain centered in problem situations
*   How to truly listen so that you can hear what you've been missing
*   And many more gems

Instantaneous Transformation
An Honest Look at Self Realization
1 hr 48 min   (ISBN: 1-888043-10-5) $19.95

Our most popular audio title now on CD.

When you hear Ariel and Shya Kane's
Instantaneous Transformation audio workshop, it could
dramatically change your life. The Kanes have found that the
slightest shift in one's reality can produce a quantum shift in
one's life. When that instant occurs, it is hard to say. You just
suddenly realize that you feel lighter, freer, more alive and that
you are interacting naturally and effectively with your present
environment. By listening to this CD, you can discover
fulfillment without working on yourself.

Magical Relationships
1 hr 51 min   (ISBN: 1-888043-06-7) $16.95

Since their first date in 1982 and subsequent
marriage in 1984, Ariel and Shya have discovered
that there are fundamental elements for finding a
relationship, and keeping it alive, exciting and
new. At this special event, taped live in New York City, the
Kanes discuss the essence of creating Magical Relationships.
By listening to this audio, you will learn the keys that are of
vital importance for getting 'em, having 'em and keeping 'em.

More...Magical Relationships
2 hrs 2 min   (ISBN: 1-888043-09-1) $16.95

Ariel and Shya's audio event, Magical
Relationships was so powerful, that people
wanted more – so here it is! By listening to these
audios, you will continue learning the keys that
are of vital importance for having all of your relationships
be exciting, fresh and satisfying. This tape expands upon
the principles of the Kanes' dramatic, new technology,
Instantaneous Transformation, in a way that you, too, can
discover how to master having truly Magical Relationships.

The Principles of Transformation
2 hrs 26 min   (ISBN: 1-888043-08-3) $16.95

In these cassettes you will learn the three fundamental principles that will facilitate personal transformation. During this extraordinary seminar, the Kanes explain and demonstrate their technology which opens the door to living in the moment. Listen to these audios and master the Principles of Transformation which will produce a quantum shift in your ability to be effective, productive and lead a highly satisfying life.

The Roots of Satisfaction
1 hr 22 min   (ISBN: 1-888043-01-6) $16.95

By listening to this dynamic audio you will discover in yourself, the 'roots of satisfaction'. You will learn to recognize and bypass the most common obstacles and misconceptions that get in the way of your self-fulfillment. You will also find out how to access and experience a state of well-being where life unfolds naturally and produces a profound sense of satisfaction.

Completing Your Karma
1 hr 23 min   (ISBN: 1-888043-07-5) $16.95

This compelling audio will help you discover how to neutralize and dissolve karma, the lingering ill effects from earlier mechanical ways of relating and behaving. This highly effective workshop outlines the keys to maximizing productivity and satisfaction. As you, too, complete your own personal karma, you will naturally have a less stressful attitude toward previously distressing situations, and a strengthened ability to be present in the moment, regardless of the circumstances.

For ordering mail to:
ASK Productions, Inc.
208 East 51st Street, PMB 137
New York, NY 10022-6500
or
via Secure Order Form at
http://www.ask-inc.com

☞ **Working on Your Relationship Doesn't Work** ___ x $ 16.95

☞ **Working on Yourself Doesn't Work** ___ x $ 12.95

☞ **Working on Yourself Doesn't Work, CD** ___ x $ 19.95

☞ **The Art of Living in the Moment, CD** ___ x $ 19.95

☞ **Instantaneous Transformation, CD** ___ x $ 19.95

☞ **Magical Relationships, Audio** ___ x $ 16.95

☞ **More...Magical Relationships, Audio** ___ x $ 16.95

☞ **The Principles of Transformation, Audio** ___ x $ 16.95

☞ **The Roots of Satisfaction, Audio** ___ x $ 16.95

☞ **Completing Your Karma, Audio** ___ x $ 16.95

Payable in U.S. funds only. No cash/COD accepted.
Postage & handling: U.S/CAN. $4.00 for one item, $1.00 for each additional, not to exeed $10.00;
International $9.00 for one item, $1.00 each additional.
We accept Visa, MC and money orders.

Bill my: ❑ Visa ❑ Mastercard _____(expires)

Card# _____

Signature _____

Bill to:

Name _____

Address _____

City _____

State, Zip, Country _____

Daytime Phone# _____

Ship to:

Name _____

Address _____

City _____

State, Zip, Country _____

Book/CD/Audio Total $ _____

NJ 6%; NY 8.625% — Sales Tax When Applicable $ _____

Postage & Handling $ _____

Total Amount Due $ _____

This offer subject to change without notice.

To read the Kanes' article of the month,
see their current schedule of events,
or to sign up to receive
Ariel and Shya's monthly newsletter,
visit their website:

WWW.ASK-INC.COM